BUGS *of* WASHINGTON *and* OREGON

John Acorn

Illustrations by Ian Sheldon

The Publisher: Lone Pine Publishing

10145-81 Ave.	202A, 1110 Seymour St.
Edmonton, AB T6E 1W9	Vancouver, BC V6B 3N3
Canada	Canada

Website: http://www.lonepinepublishing.com

National Library of Canada Cataloguing in Publication Data
Acorn, John, (date)
   Bugs of Washington and Oregon

   Includes bibliographical references and index.
   ISBN 1-55105-233-4

   1. Insects—Washington (State)—Identification. 2.
Insects—Oregon—Identification. I. Sheldon, Ian, (date) II. Title.
QL475.W38A36 2001   595.7'09795   C2001-910170-8

Editorial Director: Nancy Foulds
Project Editor: Lee Craig
Production Manager: Jody Reekie
Layout & Production: Arlana Anderson-Hale
Book Design: Heather Markham, Robert Weidemann
Cover Design: Robert Weidemann
Cover Illustration: Yellow Jacket by Ian Sheldon
Illustrations: Ian Sheldon
Photography: John Acorn
Separations & Film: Elite Lithographers Co.

The following illustrations are used with the permission of Ian Sheldon © 1999 & 2000: pp. 28–29; pp. 33–36; pp. 38–41; and pp. 43–57.

Many thanks to Great North Productions and photographer Robert van Schaik for use of the photo on p. 11.

We acknowledge the financial support of the Government of Canada through the Book Publishing Industry Development Program (BPIDP) for our publishing activities.

PC: *04*

CONTENTS

DEDICATION

To Bob Pyle and Dennis Paulson, two shining beacons of bugsterism.
Thanks to them, the entomological mystique of the Pacific Northwest has
captured many hearts, including my own.

ACKNOWLEDGMENTS

As much as I enjoyed writing this book, I enjoyed working with Ian Sheldon
even more. I can't thank Ian enough for his dedication to both the art and science of "bugs." As well, this book would not have been possible without the
characteristic generosity of many entomologists and arachnologists. In particular, Eric Coombs, Richard Westcott, James LaBonte and Richard Worth
reviewed the text and suggested many improvements, based on their long
familiarity with the Pacific Northwest fauna. Felix Sperling, George Ball and
Danny Shpeley of the University of Alberta's E.H. Strickland Entomology
Museum, as well as Brian Brown and Brian Harris of the Los Angeles County
Museum, freely provided access to reference specimens. I would also like to
thank the following people for reviewing text and graciously responding to
queries: Gary Anweiler, Brian Brown, Rob Cannings, Ed Fuller, Robert
Holmberg, Rueben Kaufman, Dave Lawrie, David Maddison, Chris Schmidt,
Ales Smetana, Terry Thormin and Daryl Williams. The staff at Lone Pine
Publishing have, as usual, been a pleasure to work with, and I would espe-
cially like to thank Lee Craig, Arlana Anderson-Hale, Robert Weidemann,
Heather Markham, Nancy Foulds and Shane Kennedy for their contribu-
tions. Finally, I would like to thank my wife Dena Stockburger and our son
Jesse for their loving support and for their enthusiasm for my work.

Western Tiger
Swallowtail, p. 28

Oregon "Old World"
Swallowtail, p. 29

Cabbage White
p. 30

Orange & Clouded
Sulphurs, p. 31

BUTTERFLIES

Spring Azure
p. 32

Purplish Copper
p. 33

Pacific Fritillary
p. 34

Great Spangled
Fritillary, p. 35

Field Crescent
p. 36

Mourning Cloak
p. 37

Painted Lady
p. 38

Red Admiral
p. 39

Lorquin's Admiral
p. 40

Common Wood
Nymph, p. 41

Monarch
p. 42

Polyphemus
Moth, p. 43

MOTHS

California Silk
Moth, p. 44

Hera Buck
Moth, p. 45

Sheep Moth
p. 46

Great Ash
Sphinx, p. 47

Big Poplar
Sphinx, p. 48

Snowberry
Clearwing, p. 49

Garden Tiger
Moth, p. 50

Carpenterworm
Moth, p. 51

Hornet Moth
p. 52

MOTHS

California Tent
Caterpillar Moth, p. 53

Yarn Moth
p. 54

Aholibah
Underwing, p. 55

Black Witch
p. 56

Spear-Marked
Black, p. 57

Pacific Tiger
Beetle, p. 58

California Tiger
Beetle, p. 59

Long-faced
Carabid, p. 60

Fiery Hunter
p. 61

BEETLES

Big Dingy Ground
Beetle, p. 62

Burying Beetle
p. 63

Hairy Rove
Beetle, p. 64

Devil's Coach
Horse, p. 65

May Beetle
p. 66

Ten-Lined June
Beetle, p. 67

Rain Beetle
p. 68

Golden Jewel
Beetle, p. 69

Western Eyed Click
Beetle, p. 70

Multicolored Asian
Ladybug, p. 71

Two-Spot Ladybug
p. 72

Convergent
Ladybug, p. 73

California Prionus
p. 74

Pine Sawyer
p. 75

Banded Alder
Borer, p. 76

Blue Milkweed
Beetle, p. 77

Blue Horntail
p. 78

Stump Stabber
p. 79

Cow Killer
p. 80

Forest Spider
Wasp, p. 81

WASPS, ANTS, BEES & SAWFLIES

Thread-Waisted
Wasp, p. 82

Golden Paper
Wasp, p. 83

Yellow Jacket
p. 84

Bumble Bee
p. 85

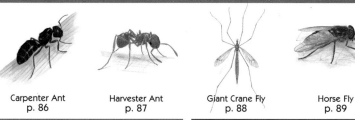

Carpenter Ant
p. 86

Harvester Ant
p. 87

Giant Crane Fly
p. 88

Horse Fly
p. 89

TWO-WINGED FLIES

7

Beeish Robber
Fly, p. 90

Hover Fly
p. 91

Drone Fly
p. 92

Green Lacewing
p. 93

TWO-WINGED FLIES

Ant Lion
p. 94

Snakefly
p. 95

Snow Scorpionfly
p. 96

Lace Bug
p. 97

LACEWINGS, SNAKEFLIES & THE LIKE

Rough Plant
Bug, p. 98

Ambush Bug
p. 99

Cicada
p. 100

Rock Crawler
p. 101

SUCKING BUGS

Road Duster
p. 102

Angular-winged
Katydid, p. 103

Field Cricket
p. 104

Cave Cricket
p. 105

GRIGS

Primitive Monster
Cricket, p. 106

Jerusalem Cricket
p. 107

Minor Ground
Mantid, p. 108

European Earwig
p. 109

MANTIDS & THE LIKE

| Giant Dampwood Termite, p. 110 | German Cockroach p. 111 | Boreal Bluet p. 112 | Common Spreadwing, p. 113 |

DRAGONFLIES & DAMSELFLIES

| Blue-eyed Darner, p. 114 | Green Darner p. 115 | Pale Snaketail p. 116 | American Emerald, p. 117 |

| Western Pondhawk, p. 118 | Common Whitetail p. 119 | Four-spotted Skimmer, p. 120 | Variegated Meadowhawk, p. 121 |

| Snow Flea p. 122 | Stream Skater p. 123 | Giant Water Bug, p. 124 | Water Boatman p. 125 | Single-banded Backswimmer, p. 126 |

SPRINGTAILS   AQUATIC ADULTS

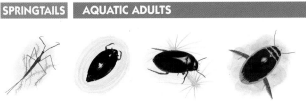

| Water Scorpion p. 127 | Whirligig Beetle p. 128 | Polished Diving Beetle, p. 129 | Giant Diving Beetles, p. 130 | Water Scavenger Beetle, p. 131 |

Salmonfly
p. 132

Mayfly Larva
p. 133

Damselfly Larva
p. 134

Dragonfly Larva
p. 135

Caddisfly Larva
p. 136

AQUATIC ADULTS **AQUATIC LARVAE**

Water Tiger
p. 137

Salmonfly Larva
p. 138

Sow Bug
p. 139

Garden Centipede
p. 140

NON-INSECT ARTHROPODS

Clown Millipede
p. 141

Scorpion
p. 142

Pseudoscorpion
p. 143

Camel Spider
p. 144

Garden Harvestman
p. 145

Carolina Wolf
Spider, p. 146

Johnson's Jumper
p. 147

Six-spotted Fishing
Spider, p. 148

Goldenrod Crab
Spider, p. 149

Black Widow
p. 150

Yellow Garden
Spider, p. 151

Long-bodied Cellar
Spider, p. 152

INTRODUCTION

This book is for bugsters. If you haven't heard the term, don't feel left out. I think I invented it with the help of my friends. We needed a word for people who are fascinated by insects, and enjoy them for no other reason than their intrinsic niftiness. "Amateur entomologist" seemed too stuffy, as did "insect enthusiast" and "entomophile." "Bugger" is out of the question. So are "bug-nut" and "bug-lover." I did find the term "entomaniac" popular among some of the people I know, but it probably isn't the best one to use as a recruiting tool. Maniacs are crazy, but we bugsters are merely enthusiastic.

Even the word "bug" is fraught with problems. In the strict language of entomology, a bug is a member of the Order Hemiptera, often pedantically called "true bugs," although I prefer the more neutral "sucking bugs" myself. The phrase "sucking bugs" refers to their sucking, not chewing, mouthparts. All other insects, including true bugs, are simply "insects." In technical language, when one expands the scope to include spiders, centipedes and millipedes, one has to resort to the phrase "terrestrial arthropods." It's tough to say that without sounding pretentious. So let's just cut through all of this confusion, and call the critters bugs, and the people who love them bugsters. These terms work for me, and the only reason they were difficult to arrive at is that our language simply hasn't been called upon to develop everyday words to go with these ideas.

The lack of a label for bugsters is odd, given the enduring appeal of bugs. Some, like butterflies, are beautiful. Others, like ladybugs and bumble bees, are familiar personalities in the garden. Then there are those bugs that are fascinating in a scary sort of way, such as spiders and scorpions. Finally, there is the wonderful diversity of insect life, and the delight that is generated by such a wide variety of living forms "right

under our noses." Biologists these days like to call this wide variety "biodiversity," and there are some who claim that people are naturally predisposed to appreciate it and crave contact with it. This idea, in turn, is called "biophilia," which can be translated as "the love of living things." I am not so sure I agree with the biophilia hypothesis, because there are so many people out there who couldn't care less about the world of plants and animals. For those who feel the connection, however, the idea of "biophilia" can be a great comfort—it makes us feel normal after all.

Of course, because not all bugs are beneficial to people, and every single one of them is smaller than a hamster, our society as a whole has developed a rather disdainful attitude toward bugs. As a consequence, most of the people who have done things to improve our understanding and appreciation of bugs have been professional biologists. Of these scientists, entomologists study insects, while arachnologists study arachnids. Those scientists who study other sorts of bugs are generally called "invertebrate zoologists," and this term can also be used to refer to the whole gang at once.

In the Pacific Northwest, as in other parts of North America, the tradition of bug study has gone on primarily in universities, as well as in research facilities operated by various levels of government. Forest and crop pests have attracted their share of attention, as have biting flies and other bugs of medical or veterinary importance. Yet some professional bugsters have studied their subjects out of "pure" fascination, and many talented and devoted amateurs have contributed to the knowledge of this region's bugs as well.

We seem poised for a resurgence of interest in our arthropod neighbors, what with a proliferation of bug-related movies, children's books and toys in the last few years. I suppose this book will probably be considered part of the same "craze," but I hope it will survive beyond that. For this reason, I have tried to make the book as entomologically correct as I could muster, while still retaining a spirit of fun and informality. I've learned, from my participation in the dinosaur craze of the 1980s, that after public attention has passed, we are still left with an interesting subject. As well, the intriguing things about it are still brought forward by the core group of people who cared about it before the fad and who will continue to care in the future.

The Pacific Northwest has about 25,000 species of bugs. This number is a guess, of course, and the reason we don't know exactly is that new species are still waiting to be discovered by science, and many species known elsewhere are here but haven't been discovered yet. Choosing the 125 "coolest" species was a challenge for me. I tried to pick bugs that are either

1) **big,**
2) **colorful,**
3) **really hard to miss or**
4) **extremely weird.**

The point of this book is to introduce you to the bugs of Washington and Oregon, not to serve as a guide to the whole kit and caboodle (whatever a "caboodle" might be). I hope you realize that to a hard-core bugster like myself, every single one of those 25,000 species has the potential to be wonderfully interesting in its own right. In other words, this book is supposed to be inspiring more than scholastic.

Before launching into the bugs themselves, let's take a moment to orient ourselves to the states of Washington and Oregon. Together, they form a roughly rectangular area, about 500 by 400 miles, taller than wide, with straight-line borders at the north and south ends. The Olympic Peninsula lies at the northern end of the western coastal border. The peninsula is dominated by Mt. Olympus, one of many gigantic volcanoes in the region.

South of the Olympic Peninsula, the Coast Ranges form a relatively low chain along the entire coast. Farther inland, and distinct from the Coast Ranges, the Cascade Range runs north and south through both states, and it forms a high, rugged mountain chain. Over the eastern portions of both states, the land slopes downward from the mountains and becomes more arid. The northern portions of this area (south of a few small mountain ranges along the Canadian border) fall broadly within the Columbia Plateau. South of the Blue and Ochoco mountains, the area becomes the Great Sandy Desert and the Harney Basin. The coast can be very moist, and the east can be very dry, but, in general, Washington and Oregon are fine places to live, with a substantial human population alongside tremendous natural resources. In other words, it is a fully modern bugsters' paradise.

BASIC BUG BANTER

Like any science, the study of bugs has its own jargon. Some of its words have plain-language equivalents, but others do not. Unavoidably, then, it is important to get the gist of things before going on to read more about the bugs themselves. I suppose I could have presented this section as a glossary, but I think it will be more interesting as a sort of condensed textbook. I hope you agree.

Bug Structure

Let's start with the structure, or anatomy, of bugs, and let's also start at the front end of an average full-grown specimen. Bugs all have a **head**, and on the head there are almost always **eyes** (with either one lens or many), a **mouth**, a set of appendages called **mouthparts** and a pair of feelers called **antennae** (one is an **antenna**). Eyes with multiple lenses are called **compound eyes**; eyes with one lens are called **ocelli** (one is an **ocellus**).

On many bugs the head is joined to the rest of the body by an obvious line or groove, and it is somewhat moveable on a flexible but very short neck.

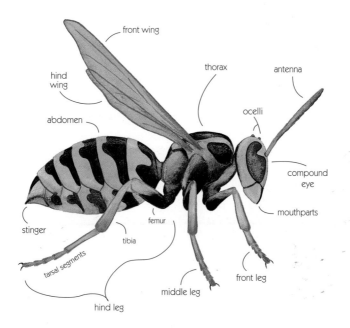

In other bugs (spiders and scorpions, for example), the head is part-and-parcel of a larger body part that also bears the legs—the **cephalothorax**. Major body parts, which is to say the head, thorax, cephalothorax or abdomen, are often further divided into **segments**, and the segments may or may not be easy to recognize on the surface.

Insects have a separate **thorax**, and it is easy to recognize because it is the part of the body that bears the legs. The thorax is, in turn, divided into three segments, each of which bears a single pair of legs. If **wings** are present, the two pairs are borne by the middle and hind segments. In many groups, the front wings are thickened and serve as wing covers for the hind wings. The three segments that make up the thorax are called the **prothorax**, **mesothorax** and **metathorax**. On beetles, the only part of the thorax that is visible from above is the prothorax, the top of which is called the **pronotum**.

Everything past the thorax is called the **abdomen**. At the tip of the abdomen, one finds the **anus**, the **reproductive structures** and, in many types of bugs, a rear-facing set of "feelers" called **cerci** (one is a **cercus**).

There are few other obvious aspects to the anatomy of a bug, but they include **spiracles** on the sides of the thorax and abdomen (openings for the multi-branched breathing tubes of insects, called the **tracheal system**) or **book lung openings** on the underside of spiders, near the silk-producing **spinnerets**. Some **aquatic** insects (insects that live in the water) have **gills** as well, most of which are leafy or finely branched projections from the body. Scorpions have comb-like sensory appendages on the underside of their cephalothorax, called **pectines**.

Life History

Now let's discuss life history. Most bugs begin life as an **egg**. The egg then hatches into a baby bug, but not all baby bugs look like their parents.

Larva   *Pupa*   *Larva*

Pupa   *Larva (nymph)*   *Naiad (larva)*

Generally, if the newly hatched young look more or less like the adults (baby grasshoppers, for example), they are likely to be called **nymphs**. If the young are clearly different from the adults, the word **larva** is more widely used (although the larvae of butterflies and moths are called **caterpillars**). Some aquatic nymphs are called **naiads**, and spider babies are simply **spiderlings**. Entomologists have recently agreed to use the word "larvae" to refer to all sorts of immature insects, but they have to fight a long history of confusion to do so. If you think this naming system is complicated, compare it to the situation with mammals, where you have to distinguish among pups, kids, calves, kits, foals, colts, lambs and so on.

As bugs grow, they have to shed their outer covering, which is called the **exoskeleton** (or more properly, the **exocuticle**), numerous times. Some bugs simply increase in size until they are large enough and mature enough to reproduce. Others show more obvious changes as they grow, the most common of which is the development of wings and **genitalia**. The genitalia are the sexual parts of bugs, and they are often complicated, involving hooks and claspers, as well as things that look like levers, pliers, syringes and the like. Sometimes the genitalia are visible from the outside and sometimes not. In spiders, one pair of mouthparts serve as the male sex organs (the **pedipalps**), and in dragonflies and damselflies the males have one set of genitalia at the tip of the abdomen and another at the base. The **base** of a structure, by the way, is always the place where it attaches to the rest of the body.

When a bug reaches the full-grown, ready-to-reproduce state, it is simply called an **adult**. However, for caterpillars and other grub-like larvae to become adults, they first have to enter into a resting stage, called the **pupa** (the plural is **pupae**), during which the amazing transformation takes place. Butterfly pupae are sometimes called **chrysalides**, and remember that the silk covering that some caterpillars make when they pupate, and not the pupa itself, is called a **cocoon**. Most cocoons come from moth caterpillars, not butterfly caterpillars.

17

The change from young to adult is called **metamorphosis**, and there are three sorts. If the change is gradual, we have "**gradual metamorphosis**." If it involves the development of wings, or some other fairly major change in body form, it is called "**incomplete metamorphosis**." If it involves a pupa stage, it is called "**complete metamorphosis**." These terms are old-fashioned and, of course, nothing is defective about an insect with "incomplete" metamorphosis.

Ecology

The ecology of bugs has to do with how they interact with other living things and with their non-living environment. The place where an insect lives is called its **habitat**, a word that means about the same as environment. All of the plants and animals in a given habitat are called a **community**, and even larger such groupings are called **ecosystems**. An insect may recognize its habitat by soil type, by slope (or flatness), by altitude, by water characteristics (flow speed, dissolved oxygen, temperature and so on) or by the presence of specific types of prey or species of plants. When insects eat plants, the plants are called **host plants** or **food plants**, and the insects are called **herbivores**. If an insect drinks nectar, the plants are called **nectar plants**. Insects that eat other creatures are **predators**, while the creatures they eat are **prey**. If an insect lives on or inside a **host** animal, and either kills it very slowly or not at all, it is called a **parasite**. If it is a parasite only in the larval stage, it is called a **parasitoid**. If an insect eats things that are already dead, it is called a **scavenger**. If it eats poop, it is said to be **coprophagous**. Complex, isn't it? Also remember that the movement of insects in one direction is called **dispersal**, while the two-way movement with the seasons is called **migration**.

There, that should do it for ecology. Now on to systematics.

Bug Systematics

Systematics is the study of how living things are related, in an **evolutionary** sense. In order to reconstruct the evolutionary tree of life, you really have to start with the basic unit of evolutionary change, the species. **Species** are groups of living things that can interbreed in nature without **hybridizing** ("crossing") with other species—at least not too much. Species are grouped with other closely related species into **genera**, the singular of which is **genus**. Genera are grouped into **families**, families into **orders**,

orders into **classes** and classes into **phyla**. This system is called **the Linnaean system of classification**. The singular of phyla is **phylum**, and all of the critters in this book belong to one phylum, the **Arthropoda** or "joint-legged animals." These creatures are what I call "bugs."

Within the phylum Arthropoda, I have chosen examples from five classes: the crustaceans (Class **Crustacea**), the millipedes (Class **Diplopoda**), the centipedes (Class **Chilopoda**), the arachnids (Class **Arachnida**) and the insects (Class **Insecta**). The arachnids are further divided into four orders in this book: the spiders (Order **Aranaea**), the harvestmen (Order **Opiliones**), the scorpions (Order **Scorpionida**) and the camel spiders (Order **Solifugae**).

Because of their great diversity, the situation with the insects is a bit more complex than with other bugs. Beginning with the flightless insects, we start with springtails, in the Order **Collembola**. These insects show gradual metamorphosis. Then we come to the insects with wings and incomplete metamorphosis: beginning with the dragonflies and damselflies in the Order **Odonata**, the mayflies in the Order **Ephemeroptera** and the stoneflies in the Order **Plecoptera**. Next come the grasshoppers, crickets and such (the **grigs**, as some people call them—the only English word for this group of insects) in the Order **Orthoptera** and the cockroaches in the Order **Dictyoptera**. Sucking bugs (the so-called true bugs) also fall into this part of the classification, and they form the Order **Hemiptera**.

The rest of the insects have complete metamorphosis, with a pupa stage. They include the two-winged flies (the "true flies") in the Order **Diptera**, the wasps, bees and ants in the Order **Hymenoptera**, the beetles in the Order **Coleoptera**, the caddisflies in the Order **Trichoptera**, the lacewings and ant lions in the Order **Neuroptera** and the butterflies and moths in the Order **Lepidoptera**.

By the way, "**ptera**" means wing, Hemiptera means half-wing, Diptera means two-wing, Lepidoptera means scaly-wing and so on. Discovering the meanings of scientific names will help you remember them, but really it is easier to just memorize the words and get on with the more

"Eyeball" Orb-weaver

19

interesting aspects of entomology. Note as well that one species is abbreviated as "sp." and many species as "spp."

In most bug books, the various groups are presented in the order that I have just given. This order places closely related groups together and begins with those species that are most **primitive** (in the sense of resembling the long-extinct common ancestor of the entire group) and ends with those that are most **derived** (a term that means they have undergone a great deal of evolutionary change). In this book, I have chosen to reverse the order. This arrangement still keeps related species together and gives you all the insight that the traditional order does, but it also allows you to start with butterflies and moths, rather than springtails. My goal is to get you to like these animals, so I have chosen to begin with the niftiest ones. At the end of the insects, however, I have "**artificially**" grouped a number of unrelated aquatic insects together in one section, because that is the way many entomologists think of them—as a unit. The non-insect bugs follow the aquatic insects.

BEING A BUGSTER

This book is not a book about pests and how to kill them. Sure, some bugs are harmful, and I don't object to fighting back against them when the need arises, so long as no other species, or people, are caught in the crossfire. But you'll find that some of my favorite bugs are pests. After all, it is always possible to admire the positive qualities of your enemies, even in the heat of battle.

Most bugs, however, are harmless, and all good bugsters know that they are the very backbone of the ecology of the Pacific Northwest, responsible for everything from pollination to decomposition, soil formation, regulation of other bugs and "weeds," food for birds and mammals and much more. Without apology, I think that all bugs are worthy of admiration and respect and at least a passing glance. If you don't understand bugs, you really don't understand the world in which you live.

Bugs are easy to find, at least on warm days during bug season, which means roughly late March through October. This long season leaves us with only four months when bugs are hard to find—pretty darn good in my opinion. Of course, May through September is the best time for bugs, during which they are downright hard to miss. Bugs live in almost every conceivable habitat, from the alpine tundra on the tops of the highest mountains to the driest prairie sand dune, the insides of caves, the insides of our homes and every place in between.

The author and his son, bug-watching

Still, if you want to go out searching for bugs, I suggest looking for them in habitats such as these:

1) under rocks and boards (and remember to put the rocks and boards back once you look),
2) on plants and especially on flowers and the undersides of leaves,
3) at lights at night (but not the yellow bug-free lights),
4) in the water, especially where there are lots of water plants,
5) on bare, sandy ground, even if it is far from water and
6) at various sorts of "bait."

My favorite bug baits include various mixtures of beer and sugar, painted on trees for moths and butterflies, as well as less appealing things such as dung and carrion. Don't feel bad if you choose to ignore the bug-baiting option. After all, many sorts of bait are downright unhygienic. Remember not to touch the bait, and always wash your hands afterwards—something my mother used to tell me often when I was a junior entomaniac.

In general, bugs like warm weather more than cool, and they are easier to find in sunny places than in shade. They prefer humid days to dry, but they don't do much in the rain. Warm nights will bring out many flying insects, such as moths, while cool nights will not. During a full moon, bugs are less attracted to lights. Wind does not necessarily deter bug activity, but it certainly makes them harder to find and to follow. Daytime bugs get going well

A Nikon 5T lens on a pair of binoculars

after we have breakfast, and they slow down appreciably by around dinner time, at least during mid-summer.

The easiest way to get a close look at a bug is to catch it, examine it, and let it go. Nets are easy to make, and good ones are also inexpensive to buy through mail-order. Small bugs can be placed in clean jars for a brief period, while large ones, such as butterflies and dragonflies, can be gently examined while they are still in the net. Many can be handled gently. In my opinion, this method is the overall best way to approach the study of bugs, and it gives a great deal of satisfaction for very little effort. All of the suggestions that follow involve more work and more of a commitment to mastering unusual techniques.

If you want to watch bugs without disturbing them, you can do it the old-fashioned way, on your elbows with a Sherlock Holmes magnifying glass, or you can try other sorts of optical tools. Close-focusing monoculars are very useful for bug-watching, but for some reason they have never really caught on among naturalists here in North America. You might also try a pair of compact binoculars, such as the Bushnell Natureview 8 × 30, with a Nikon 5T close-up lens held in front of them (total cost about $200–$250). This way, you get a clear view of the bug, at a distance of about $1^1/_2$ feet, with both eyes at once.

Depending on what sort of bug you choose to watch, your style will have to be modified. When I watch tiger beetles, I find myself crawling around on the sand, continually moving to follow my subjects. On the other hand, I often place a small folding chair in front of a buggy-looking plant, and then sit in one place while scanning the flowers, leaves and stems for interesting creatures on which to spy.

Bug-watching teaches us a lot. Because the behavior of many of our local bugs is poorly known, any of us has the ability to make useful observations once we have learned to identify the creatures we are encountering. On the other hand, simply immersing yourself in the lives of insects and other buggy critters is a wonderful way to make a deep and moving connection with the non-human world around us.

You can be as scientific or as recreational as you want. If you make detailed observations of particular sorts of insect, it is probably a good idea to collect a few "voucher specimens," so other bugsters can confirm your identifications after the fact (for really easy identifications, a close-up photograph will also suffice). When I was young, the only way to approach bug study was to make a collection. Collecting is still allowed, almost anywhere except in national and state parks, but it is no longer a popular activity.

If you choose to make a collection for educational or scientific reasons, remember to limit your catch, treat every specimen with respect, take the time to label, arrange and store the specimens correctly, and plan to donate them to a university or museum once you are done with them. Instructions for insect collecting are easy to come by, and, for the most part, you will only encounter ill-will when you collect and kill butterflies and moths—most people feel little sympathy for other sorts of bugs.

Increasingly, however, bugsters are polarizing into collecting and anti-collecting camps. I wish they weren't, but because they are, I want to briefly discuss the matter. Collectors claim they do not harm bug populations: bugs generally

have short generation times and high reproduction rates, and they recover from "harvest" much more easily than vertebrates. Collectors also point out that the identities of pinned specimens can be confirmed, whereas sightings are always subject to doubt. Anti-collectors, on the other hand, are reluctant to admit that collecting is always innocent, because they believe it *must* be

An entomologist with a research collection

possible for a large enough group of collectors to cause local extinctions of small isolated "colonies" of rare bugs. These types are exactly the sorts of bugs that many collectors seek, so this fear could be well-founded if collecting were ever to become truly popular (an unlikely possibility). Unfortunately, these isolated populations also become places where collectors and anti-collectors come into uncomfortable proximity with one another. At this point it is very difficult for the watchers to do their thing with collectors chasing the very bugs they want to observe and *vice versa*.

When I try my hardest to be rational about this subject, it seems obvious to me that insect collectors are not a big threat to the insects of the Pacific Northwest. In fact, I believe they are inconsequential. Logging, pesticides and habitat destruction are all of much greater concern. I think that the real core of the collector/anti-collector debate has to do with two rather unscientific human motives. First, no one likes having their freedom (or the freedom of their favorite bugs) restricted, especially when no laws exist to back the restrictions up. Second, collectors and anti-collectors seem to dislike the sorts of people that each other represents. Looking at these motives, let's admit that it is difficult to sympathize with those who kill the very objects of their passion. At the same time, it is hard to take people's scientific motives seriously when they are willfully unsure of the identities of the creatures they are observing and could easily remedy the situation by catching a few. It also seems clear to me that peer pressure has a great deal to do with the attitudes of individual bugsters: in a group of watchers, no one dares to bring out a net; among collectors, the binoculars stay in their cases.

As for my personal approach, I usually go out with nothing but binoculars and a camera, content to watch and admire. When I'm doing something scientific, I also take a net. I sometimes collect a specimen or two, but most of the time I use institutional collections for research. I still find many uses

Moth-catching at an illuminated bed-sheet, late at night

for pinned insects (for example, when writing this book), but I no longer feel a deep-seated need to possess them for myself. I try to act respectfully toward bugs whenever I can, but I admit that it is difficult to avoid inconsistency when you are swatting mosquitoes or splattering bugs on a windshield one moment, then treating bugs like endangered panda bears the next. This sort of "hypocrisy" is inescapable, and one can use it either to justify a callous attitude toward bugs or to accept it and atone by acting kindly toward them whenever possible.

Another fascinating bugster activity is insect rearing, which is much less controversial than collecting or watching—people who rear bugs are more or less forced to treat them with loving care, and they will inevitably acquire a specimen or two through accidental mortality. Most often, when people want to rear bugs, they start with some caterpillars and wait to see what type of butterfly or moth they will turn into. To rear caterpillars, put them in a well-ventilated cage and provide them with plenty of leaves to eat. Place the cut stems in water with some means of preventing the caterpillars from drowning in the water supply (I place soft foam around the stems). When they are ready, some caterpillars pupate above ground, but for those that dig into the soil, make sure they have some potting soil or peat to dig in when the time comes. If the pupae don't hatch in a couple of weeks, place them in the refrigerator for the winter, and mist them with water every few days (refrigerators are terribly dry places). Take them out in the spring, and don't be surprised if some pupae hatch into parasitic flies or wasps rather than butterflies or moths. Rearing caterpillars is not easy; as they grow they require more and more fresh food, and their quarters need to be cleaned frequently. If you have a lot of them, they can be almost as much effort as a new puppy!

For other insects, you will have to be more creative with your rearing techniques, but more information is becoming available on this subject all the time. Temperature, humidity, food and light, as well as making things escape-proof, are all subjects you will have to consider carefully with each new species that you try. Another popular thing to do is to set up a pond aquarium, much the same way as setting up a tropical fish tank, but without a heater.

And remember, if your bugs don't look healthy, take them back to where you caught them, and let them go.

Of course, you should not forget the potential of bug photography or even bug drawing. These activities require specialized equipment, and a certain amount of practice, but plenty of good books are on the market that can help you. With more and more sophisticated photo equipment available all the time, professional-quality bug photography is now possible with everyday equipment that you buy at an average camera store.

THE 125 COOLEST

BUGS

of

WASHINGTON & OREGON

WESTERN TIGER SWALLOWTAIL

Papilio rutulus

The Western Tiger Swallowtail is a creature of late spring and early summer. These big, bright butterflies are impressive to watch, with their soaring wing beats and graceful lines. Swallowtails are also among the few butterflies with attractive bodies—they are streamlined and luxuriantly furred in yellow and black—and even without their extravagant wings, they would be noteworthy bugs. The "tails" on a swallowtail's hind wings are there so that birds will grasp them and fly away with a beak full of membrane rather than the butterfly itself. Often, you will see a swallowtail with one or both tails missing.

There are five species of closely related North American "tiger" swallowtails, and the most famous is certainly the Eastern Tiger Swallowtail (*P. glaucus*). In that species, some females are black, to mimic the distasteful Pipevine Swallowtail (*Battus philenor*). The Pipevine Swallowtail does not occur here in the Pacific Northwest, however, except rarely in the far south, and all female Western Tiger Swallowtails are yellow like the males. The poplar-feeding caterpillars of the Western Tiger Swallowtail are amazing, too, with a fake snake-head emblazoned on a smooth, green body. The fake head draws attention away from the real head, which is small and unimpressive to look at.

WINGSPAN: about 3.3 in.
HABITAT: moist forest and shrubby regions.

OREGON "OLD WORLD" SWALLOWTAIL

Papilio machaon oregonius

T he Oregon was once considered a distinct species of swallowtail. In fact, it was very appropriately designated the state butterfly of Oregon, back in the 1970s. Lately, however, thanks to detailed studies of the relationships among swallowtails in North America, the Oregon Swallowtail has been reclassified as a geographic race of the Old World Swallowtail. This species, *Papilio machaon*, is also the most common swallowtail in Europe, where it is simply called "The Swallowtail"—because it has so few relatives on that continent. Side by side, the differences between an Oregon Swallowtail and any of the tiger-type swallowtails (the Western, Pale and Two-tailed) are obvious. In flight, however, as one flits quickly past, it is easy to confuse them. The Oregon is almost always smaller, and it has a lot more black in its wings than any of the tigers. As well, note that the tigers all have a dark line through the middle of the hind wing—something the Oregon lacks. The Oregon Swallowtail is certainly one of the most familiar butterflies in our area.

WINGSPAN: about 3 in.
HABITAT: streams and river valleys.

29

CABBAGE WHITE
Pieris rapae

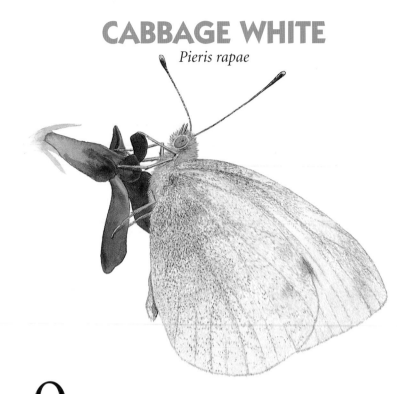

Our least-loved butterfly is another European immigrant, and its caterpillars love nothing better than to drill through defenseless greens in a suburban vegetable garden. When Europeans brought their vegetables here from the Old Country, they brought this butterfly, too. For many people the "Cabbage Moth" is the most familiar butterfly of all, and it is certainly common in the suburbs and in other places where native butterflies rarely venture. Up close, it is not a bad-looking creature, with subtle greens and yellows on a background of milky white.

The color of Cabbage Whites is a warning to birds that these butterflies taste bad, but because most of our Cabbage Whites grow up in gardens rather than among toxic wild weeds, they actually taste just fine. The similar Margined White (*P. marginalis*) lives almost exclusively in natural areas and forests, where its caterpillars feed on wild members of the mustard family. Happily, it seems that the Cabbage White and its native cousin stay out of each other's way—the country white and the city white, so to speak.

> **WINGSPAN:** about 2 in.
> **HABITAT:** gardens and agricultural areas.

ORANGE AND CLOUDED SULPHURS
Colias eurytheme & C. philodice

Sulphurs are so named because most of them are yellow. For this reason, they may also be responsible for the name "butter-fly." Of course, "butterfly" originally applied only to the sulphurs that live in Europe, most of which are quite similar to our own.

The Orange Sulphur and the Clouded Sulphur are almost identical on the underwing. On the upper wing surfaces, however, the Orange is orange, and the Clouded is yellow (see above). Both are butterflies of open, sunny meadows and fields, as well as mountain-tops and clearings. They have a direct, powerful style of flight that really doesn't fit into the category of "fluttering." Flowery fields, where they sometimes fly in

WINGSPAN: about 2 in.
HABITAT: open areas.

the thousands, are great places to find sulphurs of all sorts. These two sulphurs go through at least two generations during a typical butterfly season. The first ones to emerge are not the earliest butterflies of spring, but the last survivors are often the latest butterflies in the fall.

Over most of our area, the Orange Sulphur is the most common species of sulphur, and where additional species occur, other than the Clouded Sulphur, identifying them can be a tricky chore indeed. In fact, some of the sulphurs are probably the toughest butterflies of all to identify correctly.

SPRING AZURE
Celastrina ladon

Bluebirds are fine for some, but for those who love the smaller creatures, there is no more uplifting sight than the year's first Spring Azure. Flashing and dodging, close to the ground, this lovely little butterfly is as iridescent as a tropical parrot and as bright as the April skies above. Later in the season, other species of "blues" will appear, with darker blue colors and more crisply marked underwings, but the Spring Azure is the one that comes out first, making it the species we know and love the best.

In fact, the Spring Azure is usually the first butterfly of the year to emerge from its pupa. Most of the other spring butterflies, such as Mourning Cloaks and Tortoiseshells, have spent the winter as adult butterflies, tucked away under bark or among deadfall. By the time late spring rolls around, the last of the azures are looking gray and weather beaten. Most butterflies live only a week or two as adults, and their brief lives are usually squandered at the expense of their diminutive beauty. It is the males we see most often— they fly whenever the sun is out, searching for females.

WINGSPAN: about 1 in.
HABITAT: forest clearings and open areas.

PURPLISH COPPER

Lycaena helloides

Anyone who takes an interest in butterflies will soon find that the subject is inexhaustible. Just when you think you have encountered all of the butterfly types in your area, you notice a small, inconspicuous one, low to the ground. Most of the time, this butterfly will be a copper, and it is a delight. Most of our coppers are at least partly orange, and a combination of orange-and-brown markings

> **WINGSPAN:** about 1 in.
> **HABITAT:** open areas and clearings, especially moist ones.

does, indeed, give them a semi-coppery look, but none of the coppers look as much like copper as a good copper-colored beetle (butterfly names being what they are).

The most common species of copper in our area is probably the Purplish Copper, and it is the males that have a purple iridescence. Purplish Coppers first appear in mid-summer, and in a warm year they can also have a second generation that emerges in the early fall. This second generation can be just as abundant as the first, and the coppers are often seen in suburban neighborhoods or on the borders of cornfields.

PACIFIC FRITILLARY

Boloria epithore

Fritillary is a confusing word. It refers to a large assortment of orange-and-black butterflies, and it can be pronounced either "FRIT-ill-erry" or "frit-TILL-err-ee." To make things more complicated, there are also flowers called "fritillaries," and in Europe all sorts of semi-related butterflies are called "fritillaries." The Pacific Fritillary is one of the so-called "lesser fritillaries," which are generally smaller than the greater fritillaries. As well, few of the lesser fritillaries have silver spots on their underwings (and the Pacific Fritillary has none).

A number of species of lesser fritillaries emerge throughout the butterfly season, and they are easy to find, because most of them have the enchanting habit of feeding while spreading their wings wide open to the sun. For this reason, they also make great subjects for nature photography. Some of these fritillaries live in meadows in the forested regions, while others range far into the alpine zone at the tops of mountains. To tell a Pacific Fritillary from the other lesser "frits," one has to memorize the exact pattern of splotches on the underside of the hind wing—a fairly standard thing to do once you become a "hard-core" butterflier.

WINGSPAN: about 1.4 in.
HABITAT: widespread in meadows and clearings.

GREAT SPANGLED FRITILLARY
Speyeria cybele

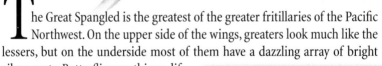

The Great Spangled is the greatest of the greater fritillaries of the Pacific Northwest. On the upper side of the wings, greaters look much like the lessers, but on the underside most of them have a dazzling array of bright silver spots. Butterflies see things differently than people, and much of what they see lies in the ultraviolet range, so these spots are bright ultraviolet beacons to other fritillaries. At a distance, fritillaries attract one another with their appearance, but when they get close, they choose to communicate with perfumes instead. Sound familiar?

WINGSPAN: about 2.4 in.
HABITAT: forest openings.

Fritillary caterpillars, by the way, feed on the leaves of violets, and they only come out at night. In mid-summer, when the air is filled with fritillaries, but the violets have finished blooming, you wouldn't think that there were enough violet leaves to go around. For those bugsters who like identification challenges, the greater fritillaries fit the bill perfectly. Many species are in our area, and some of them are so similar to one another that even experts can't seem to agree on what name to use.

FIELD CRESCENT
Phyciodes campestris

Tiny, bright and proud—that's how I think of crescents. These butterflies are small, but they fly with the grace and assurance of a majestic
Monarch (p. 42). Sometimes, they even glide, which is quite a feat at their
size. Crescents are the smallest members of the brush-footed butterfly family
(named for the tiny, brush-like front legs). Brush-foots walk on only four
legs, and really, they don't walk much at all. Because their middle and hind
legs serve perfectly well to hold the body steady when they are at rest, the
front legs have virtually disappeared through the process of evolution.

WINGSPAN: about 1.2 in.
HABITAT: meadows and clearings.

Crescents like to perch on a sunlit leaf and spread their intricately
patterned wings to the sky. You get a
great look at their features, but it
doesn't mean they are easy to identify—there are a number of species of
amazingly similar crescents. As well, it is often the underside of the wing that
bears the distinguishing marks. Don't let this identification problem discourage you from enjoying them, however. Where there are shrubs to perch
on, crescents are easy to find, and their "personality"—if butterflies can have
a personality—more than makes up for their size.

MOURNING CLOAK
Nymphalis antiopa

The Mourning Cloak is a big, heavy-bodied, spectacular butterfly. You can hope to see one almost any sunny day that the temperature rises above freezing, even in winter. The adults emerge from their pupae in mid- to late summer, at which point they are at their most magnificent: maroon with yellow trim and blazing blue highlights, with a bark-colored pattern on the underside. After feeding for a week or so, they go into a temporary dormancy and then emerge to feed again in the fall. When the snow comes, they tuck in under a chunk of bark, a shutter or a fallen log and hibernate. Sometimes they die during hibernation, and you find their remains when you clean out the attic or the woodpile.

WINGSPAN: about 3.1 in.
HABITAT: openings in forested areas.

The first warm days of spring bring them back out of hiding, and that's when they mate and lay eggs. By the time early summer rolls around, a few are still on the wing—worn and tattered, with white wing fringes instead of yellow. A Mourning Cloak can live a full year, which is almost a year longer than most other butterflies.

PAINTED LADY
Vanessa cardui

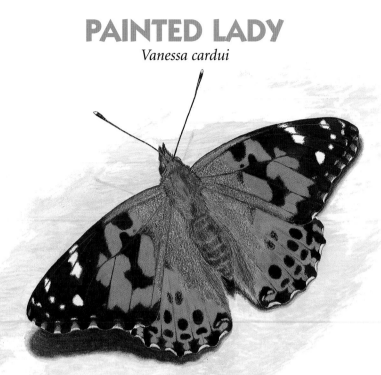

A lovely orange, black and white butterfly, swift on the wing and with a love for thistles—that's a Painted Lady. Often, I hear people say that these butterflies used to be very common in the good old days, but now they have all but disappeared. Well, in some places that might be true. Usually, however, these people are recalling a time when Painted Ladies arrived on migration, which is something that happens only once every 10 or so years.

The populations of these butterflies build up in the southern U.S. over the course of a decade, at which point they swarm up into the north by the bazillions. No thistle is safe from the egg-laying females, and a northern generation grows up over the summer. These butterflies don't realize that they should return south in the fall (or at least most of them don't). When winter arrives, they die in droves.

WINGSPAN: about 2.2 in.
HABITAT: open areas.

In Washington and Oregon, we also see the very similar West Coast Lady (*V. annabella*) and the American Lady (*V. virginiensis*), both of which can be easily confused with the Painted Lady.

RED ADMIRAL
Vanessa atalanta

The Red Admiral, a close cousin to the Painted Lady (p. 38), is also a migratory species, and it is only common every once in a while (usually every seven years or so). Unlike the ladies, however, Red Admiral caterpillars do not eat thistles—they eat nettles. So, you really have to admire the contribution that these butterflies make to our summer environment. I also like the way they choose a sunlit patch of ground and patrol it at high speed between basking periods on the ground or a tree trunk. They appear to be territorial and defend their favorite area vigorously against intruders, be they other admirals or not.

> **WINGSPAN:** about 2 in.
> **HABITAT:** open areas and openings in forested areas.

Up close, you can see that this butterfly has a thick body, powerful flight muscles and stout, angular wings for rapid, super-controlled flight. When you find one in the spring, it is usually quite worn and dull, with wing markings that are closer to pale orange than red. But when the summer generation emerges, the colors are dark and saturated, and the body is clothed in thick, brown hairs.

LORQUIN'S ADMIRAL
Liminitis lorquini

A large, black butterfly with a white band through the middle of both sets of wings pretty much has to be an admiral. The Lorquin's Admiral is a characteristic western species, easy to recognize because of the orange suffusion on the tips of the front wings. Entomologists seem to like the word "suffusion," which implies a certain blurriness, and it's a word that often comes in handy when describing insect colors. The name "Admiral," by the way, was originally "Admirable," which makes good sense—too bad it faded from use.

The Lorquin's Admiral is typical of its group in that it is often found sunning on either the ground or on vegetation, and it is also a common sight on muddy roads, where it sips for nutrients. Apparently, when butterflies feed on mud, they are primarily after sodium, because sodium is

WINGSPAN: about 2.6 in.
HABITAT: forest openings.

hard to get from flower nectar alone (which is not to say that flower nectar is simple sugar water—it's not). As well, admirals will sometimes sip at the most disgusting of wet things, including dead animals, dung and places where people or other animals have recently urinated.

COMMON WOOD NYMPH
Cercyonis pegala

You've probably already seen this butterfly but have given it little thought. Just about any grassy field in mid-summer will have at least a few Common Wood Nymphs fluttering around at about the height of the tallest seed heads. Follow one, and you'll soon give up on getting a better look—this butterfly almost never sits still, and you rarely see it at a flower. Like all other butterflies, however, it has to sleep.

The sun comes up early in summer, and the birds come up with it, searching for food among the dew-covered meadows. Wood nymphs, like other butterflies, don't start flying until much later in the morning—sometimes not until 10 a.m. or so—forcing them to spend quite some time sitting in the open, hoping they don't get eaten. That's why they have a set of fake eyespots on their forewings that can be flashed at a predator if the need arises. Birds are not too bright, and they often fall for the bluff, thinking they have disturbed the slumber of some glassy-eyed reptile. It really is too bad that these butterflies are not more inclined to show off their wings, because the males have a lovely, purplish iridescence.

> **WINGSPAN:** about 2.4 in.
> **HABITAT:** grassy areas, including open woodlands.

41

MONARCH
Danaus plexippus

The Monarch is our most famous butterfly and one of our biggest as well. Most people know the story: the Monarch is a migrant, and individuals born in our area travel each winter to a few small areas in northern and central California, where they spend the winter alongside the rest of the Monarchs from the West Coast of North America. No one quite knows how they find their traditional wintering grounds, having never been there, but they do. Sadly, all of their wintering areas are threatened by development.

Monarchs make this great migration against huge odds, but they are partly protected by their body chemistry. As a caterpillar, each Monarch feeds on the leaves of milkweed plants, and chemicals in the leaves make both the caterpillar and the butterfly distasteful to birds. The distinctive orange and black colors on the Monarch advertise this defense; another butterfly copies these colors to help protect itself. This butterfly is, of course, the Viceroy (*Liminitis archippus*). A Viceroy is smaller than the Monarch (the wingspan is only about 2.8 in), but the birds don't seem to notice. The Monarch is not common here, and it is found mainly in northeast Oregon and southwest Washington State.

WINGSPAN: about 3.7 in.
HABITAT: open areas near milkweed.

POLYPHEMUS MOTH

Antheraea polyphemus

When a Polyphemus Moth comes flapping in to the porch light, everyone takes notice. Many people assume this moth is a butterfly, because it is so amazingly beautiful. The antennae tell the real story—fuzzy or thin and pointy antennae all belong to moths, while butterflies have slender antennae with thickened tips. The antennae of male moths are not feelers but smellers, and they pick up the faint aroma of a female's perfume. Following the scent upwind, the male finds his mate in the dark.

When daylight comes, Polyphemus Moths generally roost with their wings above their backs. If a bird tries to peck at them, they suddenly spread the wings to expose the fake eyes on the wings. Most birds are startled by this display, but it doesn't fool every predator. Often, all you find of a Polyphemus is a pile of wings on the ground in the morning. The name "Polyphemus" comes from a one-eyed giant in Greek mythology; too bad the moth has four fake eyes and two real ones, for a total of six. Polyphemus caterpillars, by the way, are bright green and shaped like an extended accordion, and they feed on such things as birch and dogwood leaves.

WINGSPAN: about 4.3 in.
HABITAT: deciduous forests.

43

CALIFORNIA SILK MOTH
Hyalophora euryalus

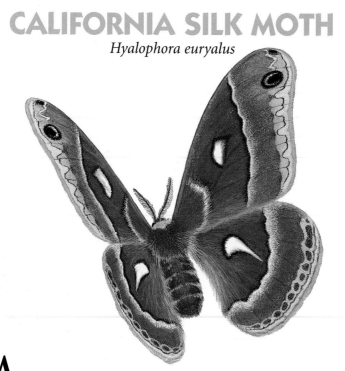

About the same size as a Polyphemus Moth (p. 43), the California Silk Moth is less common. As such, it generates even more excitement when it appears around people. Both the California and the Polyphemus are members of the giant silkworm family, a separate group from the commercial silkworms of Asia. At one point, the possibility of using giant silkworms for making silk to sell was explored in North America. It turned out that they wrap too many leaves and messy knots into their cocoons, so the plan failed. Thus, the giant silkworms remain symbols of the wild.

WINGSPAN: about 3.9 in.
HABITAT: shrubby areas.

In more populated regions, California Silk Moths are gradually decreasing in numbers as habitat is destroyed and moths spend their lives flapping around light bulbs, instead of mating and laying eggs. Adult giant silkworms are among the bugs that have no mouth and live off body reserves once they emerge from the pupae. If you find one and it poops a light brown liquid, don't be alarmed. The liquid is "meconium" and consists of the wastes left over from the transformation from caterpillar to moth. This moth is often misidentified as the similar Cecropia Moth (*H. cecropia*) that only lives in eastern North America.

HERA BUCK MOTH
Hemileuca hera

The buck moths are also members of the giant silkworm family, despite the fact that they are not particularly gigantic. They are, however, very boldly patterned in black and white, with furry bodies that have bright red and yellow tufts

WINGSPAN: about 2.4 in.
HABITAT: open, arid areas.

of hairs. Most often, people notice them as they rest on vegetation near ground level, often in the act of mating. They are day-flying moths—active in sunshine—and their flight is fast and frantic. The caterpillars feed on various sorts of sagebrush leaves, and the hairs on their bodies can sting you if you touch them. The result is a temporary rash—a reminder that hairy caterpillars are not always safe to handle, no matter how cute they might appear. In other parts of the world, some caterpillars can send you to the hospital.

As you go further south, the number of buck moth species increases to about 18, and they are the most diverse group within the giant silkworm moth family here in North America. The American Southwest is the buck moth hot spot, and bugsters are still struggling to discover how many species there are, and how to classify them.

45

SHEEP MOTH
Hemileuca eglanterina

The Sheep Moth is a type of buck moth (a member of the genus *Hemileuca*), and like others in this group, it flies by day. Older books place this species in a separate genus, *Pseudohazis*, because it isn't a typical-looking buck moth. It has broader wings and a slimmer body, and this combination makes the Sheep Moth look a lot like a butterfly at first glance. Still, Sheep Moths have furry antennae—a sure sign that they are moths and not butterflies—and although they are active during the day, they still rely heavily on chemical communication to find their mates (the antennae are used to smell for prospective partners).

WINGSPAN: 2–2.6 in.
HABITAT: open areas.

Compared to the Hera Buck Moth (p. 45), this species has a much more intricate wing pattern, with "sunburst" edges and thick, graceful, black lines through the wings. The Sheep Moth is also highly variable in color: some individuals are almost pure black and white, while others are a deep orange color overall. Color variation is common among moths and butterflies, and it can serve a number of different functions, related mainly to courtship, camouflage or mimicry. In the case of the Sheep Moth, we still do not know which explanation is correct. Watch for the Sheep Moth in late summer on warm afternoons, flying high above the ground.

GREAT ASH SPHINX
Sphinx chersis

S phinx moths are named for the way their caterpillars adopt a pose something like the famous Sphinx of Egypt. Another name for this group is "hawk moths," based on their streamlined form and rapid flight. I prefer "sphinx," because moths, unlike hawks, are not predators. In fact, they feed on flower nectar. There are many sorts of flowers that open their petals and produce nectar at night, to accommodate these nocturnal pollinators. The proboscises of sphinx moths can be extraordinarily long— sometimes longer than the body, sometimes twice as long or more!

The Great Ash Sphinx is one of the largest in the Pacific Northwest, and it is a fairly typical member of the family. Despite its name, its caterpillars are not exclusively found on ash leaves. They will feed on a variety of tree species, including lilac, quaking aspen and cherry. The caterpillars are huge, of course, and they never fail to attract attention as they march across roads and sidewalks on their way to a place to dig into the soil and form pupae. While the Great Ash is never a common moth, it is always interesting and exciting to see.

WINGSPAN: about 4.3 in.
HABITAT: shrubby and treed areas.

BIG POPLAR SPHINX
Pachysphinx modesta

A large female Big Poplar Sphinx probably has the heaviest body of any moth in Washington or Oregon, and this species' caterpillar certainly qualifies as one of our biggest insects overall. The Big Poplar Sphinx is an uncommon find, and even experienced moth devotees are always thrilled when they see one. Most sphinx moths feed on flower nectar, but some, like the Big Poplar, are unable to feed as adults. The Big Poplar has no mouth, and in this way it resembles giant silkworm moths (pp. 43–46).

The Big Poplar Sphinx also has fairly broad wings for a sphinx, patterned in subtle pastel hues, camouflaged on the front wings and smeared with blue and red on the hind wings. The outer border of the front wings is wavy, which undoubtedly helps camouflage these moths during the day. The eyes are difficult to see, hidden by the furry forehead and shoulders, and the combination of all these features probably gave this bug its scientific name, which is often translated as "Modest Sphinx." This name brings up an important point: bugs do not seem to possess a self-image, or anything we might recognize as an ego. At least, no one has ever produced any evidence to support the notion. Thus, without an ego, I doubt it is possible for any bug to be either modest, conceited or anything in between.

> **WINGSPAN:** about 4.3 in.
> **HABITAT:** forests with poplars.

SNOWBERRY CLEARWING
Hemaris diffinis

Another name for this little creature is the "Hummingbird Moth." Sure enough, when it hovers in front of a flower, uncoils the long, beak-like proboscis, and shows off its handsome colors, you can see why some people think they are looking at a bird. In bird field guides, this moth is usually the only insect that warrants a picture. More than one friend of mine

> **WINGSPAN:** about 1.6 in.
> **HABITAT:** open areas throughout the region.

has told me that the first time they saw one, they crept up for a better look and then felt a deep sense of dread, realizing they had no idea what sort of life-form they were looking at.

Of course, there is nothing to fear about these moths, and, in fact, they are quite delightful. They are members of the sphinx moth family, and they behave like most of their nocturnal cousins. The see-through wings and daytime habits are the only things that set them apart from their relatives. Typical of sphinxes, the caterpillars feed on a variety of forest plants. The adult moths are on the wing mainly in May. There are two, possibly three species of very similar clear-winged sphinxes in our area, of which the Snowberry Clearwing is the most common.

GARDEN TIGER MOTH
Arctia caja

T iger moths are not especially big, but they include some of the prettiest moths of all. The Garden Tiger Moth is one of the largest in Washington and Oregon. In a good year it is easy to find. Like many insects, its population fluctuates greatly from year to year, easily able to bounce back from a bad year or two because the females lay huge numbers of eggs. The most important thing determining the number of moths in a given year is the number of caterpillars that survive the early life history of the species.

The bright colors of tiger moths exist to warn predators not to eat them—they are filled with bad-tasting chemicals. Of course, their warning colors only work during the day. At night, the main enemies of tiger moths are bats, so they must defend themselves in other ways. Some tiger moths can hear the bats coming, way above the range of human hearing.

WINGSPAN: about 2.2 in.
HABITAT: forested areas.

When a tiger moth feels threatened, it makes its own ultrasonic sounds, to warn the bat that it is about to get a mouthful of bad-tasting tiger moth. Tiger moth caterpillars are generally fuzzy, and the fuzz can cause itchiness and rashes. They even weave these hairs into their cocoons, meaning that the insect is protected at every stage of its life, both day and night.

CARPENTERWORM MOTH
Prionoxystus robiniae

T wo things set the Carpenterworm apart from most of the Pacific Northwest's other familiar moths. First, it shows "sexual dimorphism." Sexual dimorphism is the standard scientific term for differences in the appearance of males and females. In the Carpenterworm Moth, the male is small and has streamlined, pointed wings, like a sphinx moth (pp. 47–49). As well, the male's wings are more darkly mottled, and his hind wings are yellow. The female (shown above) is larger, with broader wings and a

WINGSPAN: females about 2.8 in or more; males smaller.
HABITAT: southern forests.

translucent gray pattern. Most likely, the male is adapted to find the female from a distance, while the female is more of an egg-laying specialist. The second thing that sets this moth apart from other moths in this area is that its caterpillars eat wood, not leaves. The caterpillars of these moths dig tunnels in the wood of deciduous trees, and, as you can imagine, they are large creatures. People often discover them when splitting firewood.

Moth specialists often divide the moths into the "macro-moths" and the "micro-moths," and, for the most part, the micros are indeed smaller than the macros. The Carpenterworm, however, is the biggest of our micros, and a big female can have a wingspan of 3.3 inches, dwarfing the vast majority of macro-moths. Such is the power of tradition, where unsuitable names persist despite their obvious flaws.

HORNET MOTH
Sesia apiformis

The Hornet Moth is a member of another very impressive group of "micro-moths": the clear-winged moths, which almost all look like wasps. The Hornet Moth itself is a mimic of the paper wasps (p. 83), but other species of clear-winged moths mimic a variety of smaller stinging wasps. At a distance, it is not always easy to tell a Hornet Moth from a real wasp. Look for a slightly dumpier body, with a furry look rather than smooth—that's the moth.

I have not seen any studies on the subject, but it is possible that the mimicry goes both ways in this case. Whereas wasps have a painful sting, many members of the clear-winged moth family possess distasteful chemicals, and some are known to purposely extract these chemicals from plants by regurgitating onto bark and repeatedly sucking up their own digestive juices. So perhaps, as far as the birds are concerned, both Hornet Moths and hornets are to be avoided, and having only one color pattern to remember helps them do this more easily.

WINGSPAN: about 1.4 in.
HABITAT: shrubby areas.

Hornet Moth caterpillars, like the caterpillars of Carpenterworm Moths (p. 51), feed inside wood and roots, mostly on poplars and willows. The moths are generally more common than one might think, because they go undetected most of the time.

CALIFORNIA TENT CATERPILLAR MOTH
Malacosoma californicum

This moth is probably best known as a caterpillar. The moth itself is not unattractive—furry and brown—but it takes an expert eye to recognize that it is a member of a relatively small family of furry, brown moths, the lappet moth family (Lasiocampidae). Most other furry, brown moths are either owlet moths (Family Noctuidae) or prominent moths (Family Notodontidae).

This species takes its name from the habits of its caterpillars. The mother moth lays her eggs all together in an egg mass, and when the caterpillars hatch they stay together as a little, furry family. They spin a silk shelter for themselves, in which they spend the daylight hours safe from birds and parasites. At night they venture out to feed on leaves, usually of poplars and willows. When they are ready to pupate, they wander away from the tent, and spin a cocoon about the size and shape of a perogie or a Japanese dumpling. Some years there are huge numbers of tent caterpillars, and they

> **WINGSPAN:** about 1.4 in.
> **HABITAT:** widespread in deciduous forests.

can be important pests, while other years they are rare. Parasitic flies and wasps, along with diseases, cause these tremendous fluctuations in numbers.

53

YARN MOTH

Tolype spp.

T he Yarn Moth belongs to the same family as the tent caterpillar moth (p. 53), but it is likely that most people would consider the Yarn Moth by far the more elegant of the two. A fresh specimen does indeed look a bit "yarnish," with long, bright white and brown hairs on its thorax and abdomen. This moth is one of those that impresses people easily, because it looks so terribly warm and fuzzy. The hairs on the body seem to form a sort of mane, while the very hairy legs make this moth look like either a white tarantula or a Persian cat, depending on your sense of moth aesthetics. Almost all the Yarn Moths we see are males that have been attracted to lights.

WINGSPAN: about 1 in.
HABITAT: forested areas.

The Yarn Moths are found in forested areas—their caterpillars feed on tree leaves of various sorts. Oddly enough, some species feed on conifer needles while others feed on deciduous tree leaves. In most groups of moths, closely related caterpillars feed on closely related plants, but they don't always do so, nor is this a tremendously mysterious phenomenon. The caterpillars of Yarn Moths are not economic pests.

AHOLIBAH UNDERWING
Catocala aholibah

The underwings are the moths of late summer. On occasion you see them by day, but for the most part they are creatures of the early evening, when they search for the sap-flows and over-ripe fruit on which they feed. Their coloration is remarkable, with camouflaged front wings and boldly colored hind wings. At rest, the Aholibah Underwing blends in perfectly with tree bark by closing its front wings over the hind ones. If a bird discovers it, the moth spreads its wings and takes advantage of the brief startle effect to allow it a moment in which to escape.

WINGSPAN: about 2.6 in.
HABITAT: deciduous forests.

If you want to see one of these moths, here's what to do: mix up a pot of beer, molasses, rum and lots of brown sugar; warm it up to melt the sugar, then let it cool; go outside and paint the mixture on the rough bark of poplar trees, then wait until after dark; and finally, sneak up carefully with a flashlight, and try not to snap any twigs. Moths have good hearing, and they will sometimes flee at the slightest sound. Of course, after an hour or so of sipping the alcoholic bait, they seem less concerned about people, and more absorbed in their own inebriated thoughts. This technique, by the way, seems to work much better in the eastern states than here in the west, much to the chagrin of local bugsters.

BLACK WITCH

Ascalapha odorata

The Black Witch is our largest moth, but it's not really "ours" in a way. Every summer, a few of these impressive creatures turn up in the Pacific Northwest, flying to lights. Would you believe that each one of these was born somewhere in Central America? This tropical species disperses widely in all directions each and every year. On powerful elongated wings, these moths make their way north, becoming less and less common the further north they go. It shouldn't surprise anyone to notice that the ones we find here are generally worn and faded, with torn wing edges and dull colors.

WINGSPAN: up to 6 in.
HABITAT: forested areas.

To fuel such a journey (longer, by the way, than the flight of a Monarch butterfly to its wintering grounds in California), the moths feed each night at sap or rotting fruit. Thus, they are drawn to the same sorts of bait that attract underwings (p. 55), and actually, they are the largest members of the underwing subfamily of the owlet moths. Don't let their lack of a colorful hind wing fool you—they are still closely related. Males have longer, more pointed wings, while females have a light band through the middle of the wings.

SPEAR-MARKED BLACK
Rheumaptera hastata

The wings of this familiar moth are patterned in black and white, with a delicately curvaceous outer margin. The moth's relatively light body struggles to flap the wings, and thus it doesn't whir in flight like most moths. Instead, it flutters. In fact, there are only three sure signs that this one is not a butterfly. First, it has thin antennae with no clubs at the tips. Second, it flies by night. Third, it has a habit of crashing into leaves and branches when it flies, rather than deftly avoiding them.

The Spear-marked Black is a member of a large group of equally enchanting moths, the "geometers." These moths are also called "inchworm moths," because their caterpillars perform the familiar inching-along motion when they travel. Their method of locomotion is also respon-

WINGSPAN: about 1.4 in.
HABITAT: forested areas.

sible for the names "looper" and "spanworm." Many of the geometers are colorful, and some, such as the Spear-marked Black, also fly by day. Almost always, when someone comes to me with a "butterfly that isn't in the field guides," it turns out to be a geometer.

PACIFIC TIGER BEETLE

Cicindela oregona

Tiger beetles are exciting: they have long legs, they run fast, they have powerful jaws for killing other bugs, and they also have large eyes. Some tiger beetles, as an added bonus, are brightly colored. The Pacific Tiger Beetle is widespread and common, but it is really one of the least colorful members of the group (pp. 58–59). These beetles live on moist sand and gravel, alongside both lakes and rivers. They generally like open ground with few plants; they find it easy in such places to spot prey and run it down.

It's a shame more people don't get a chance to see tiger beetles, but the reason is simple—the beetles always see us first. However, don't despair! They are quick to take wing but usually don't fly far. It's easy to watch where they land and sneak up for a good look. If you watch a tiger beetle, you'll see it chase down food, zip out after potential mates and attack any small piece of debris that might be an edible bug. These beetles only come out on sunny days, mind you, so don't go looking for them in the rain—that's the time to stick to water beetles.

LENGTH: 0.5 in.
HABITAT: widespread on riverbanks and beaches.

CALIFORNIA TIGER BEETLE

Omus californicus

T his tiger beetle is a sort of missing link. With small eyes, nocturnal habits and a much slower running speed, this one acts much like a ground beetle, instead of a tiger beetle. It is also colored like a ground beetle, all black with no white markings or iridescence. These similarities, plus others, have caused many specialists to declare that tiger beetles form a

LENGTH: about 0.6 in.
HABITAT: forest clearings.

subgroup within the ground beetle family. However, the California Tiger Beetle also possesses a type of jaw that is unique to tiger beetles, and its larvae are very typically tiger-beetlish as well.

This beetle lives in vertical burrows in the ground and ambushes small bugs that walk by. No intermediate jaws or larvae are known, either living or fossil, to connect the tiger beetles and the ground beetles. Thus, it is also possible that tiger beetles form an ancient lineage separate from ground beetles. They are a worldwide group, ranging in size and shape from big-eyed, tiny, tree-dwelling species to huge, long-jawed, nocturnal tigers in South Africa. And the solution to the problem of classifying them might live right here, with the California Tiger Beetle and its kin.

LONG-FACED CARABID
Scaphinotus angusticollis

N ext time you are out camping in the moist coastal forests, spend a few extra minutes looking around with your flashlight when you make that inevitable trip to the outhouse after dark. Over much of the summer, you can expect to find a large, brownish-black ground beetle prowling the forest floor. This beetle is the Long-faced Carabid, and it is an elegant beetle indeed. With an elongated head, a remarkably slender prothorax and a body shaped like a cartoon rowboat, it is not your average ground beetle. Of course, there is no such thing as an average ground beetle, because in most places there are about as many species of ground beetles as there are kinds of birds. You wouldn't talk about an average bird, would you, halfway between a hummingbird and a pelican?

LENGTH: 0.9 in.
HABITAT: moist coastal forests.

Long-faced Carabids are thought to be adapted to eating snails and slugs—their long heads help them get into those hard-to-reach places in snail shells and massive banana slug carcasses. However, the observations of local naturalists show that they will also feed on a variety of other small bugs, as well as on fallen fruit.

60

FIERY HUNTER
Calosoma calidum

H ere is another sort of ground beetle, with its own fascinating story. Like the Long-faced Carabid (p. 60), this beetle is one of the larger members of the family, but it differs from the Long-faced in both its looks and habits. The Fiery Hunter has hundreds of ruby red jewel spots set in its shining, black wing covers. These spots really do look like jewels, even under a magnifying glass. As well, notice that you will sometimes find Fiery Hunters with green or golden, rather than red, jewel spots, and that these ones are not a different species, just a different variation on a lovely little theme.

LENGTH: 0.9 in.
HABITAT: forests.

While the Long-faced Carabid likes to rummage around on the forest floor, the Fiery Hunter is also a fearless climber of trees. Day and night, it explores the woods for its favorite food—caterpillars. Even fuzzy tent caterpillars are to its liking. With its mighty jaws and a head as hard as a chokecherry pit, the Fiery Hunter chews through a caterpillar's hairy defenses and gobbles up the soft insides. This species is uncommon in our area, found most often in the east.

BIG DINGY GROUND BEETLE

Harpalus pennsylvanicus

T his ground beetle is by no means our biggest or most spectacular, but it's one that everyone should know. When you think that the average size of a beetle is about 0.09 inches, the Big Dingy takes its rightful place as one of the whoppers. In its appearance, this ground beetle is what biologists call "generalized." In other words, it doesn't possess any obvious body features that constitute adaptations for a specialized lifestyle (for example, the elongate head of a Long-faced Carabid, p. 60). However, the Big Dingy is not a primitive ground beetle—it is more likely that the Fiery Hunter (p. 61) resembles the long-extinct ancestor of the ground beetle group. Because there are so many ground beetles, many people have made it their entomological mission to study this group. Luckily, I have been able to meet many of the living "carabidologists" myself. There is a rumor among these people that the so-called "dingy" ground beetles (technically, the "harpalines") were given their common name by specialists in other sorts of ground beetles, as a playful dig at those who study the "dingy" ones.

LENGTH: 0.5 in.
HABITAT: open, drier areas.

BURYING BEETLE
Nicrophorus spp.

Somebody has to deal with them, and you know exactly what I am talking about. Yes, I'm referring to dead mice. Without nature's help, the world would be knee deep in them. That is where beautiful Burying Beetles (most are orange and black, while others are all black) fit into the grand scheme of things. Flying low over the ground, just before sundown, they spread their many-leaved antennae to the wind and sniff. They seek the unmistakable aroma of today's death. If they find a big carcass, such as a deer or a coyote, they join their buddies for a quick snack. On the other hand, if they find a dead mouse, or some other tiny corpse, they rejoice. A

LENGTH: 0.6 in.
HABITAT: large variety, mostly open areas.

Burying Beetle's dream is to find a dead mouse and a mate all in the same evening. Then, the couple can bury the treasure, kill the maggots that might steal some of the meal, and push the cadaver into a ball. Next, they lay their own eggs, and start a family. The beetle grubs raise their little heads to beg for food, and in response Mom and Dad give them bits of putrescence to eat. Now isn't that nice? Who said that beetles don't possess the ability to show complex behavior and tender parental care?

HAIRY ROVE BEETLE

Creophilus maxillosus

Rove beetles form a diverse family of beetles, but most are very small. To the majority of people, a rove beetle doesn't look much like a beetle at all. The Hairy Rove Beetle is a large, elongate, slender insect, and its wing covers are short. A beetle it is, however, and a good one at that. Beneath those wing covers are full-sized wings, folded so intricately that you'd swear they couldn't fit.

The Hairy Rove Beetle is another bug that is attracted to death. Any carcass will do, and these beetles are some of the first insects to arrive after decomposition has set in. The Hairy Rove Beetle is not there to eat the meat, mind you. Instead, it is there to ambush the unwary. After all, a dead animal is a magnet for bugs. So the Hairy Rove Beetle prowls the cadaver and dines on flies, maggots and various other beetles.

LENGTH: up to 0.9 in.
HABITAT: attracted to carrion, mainly in open areas.

The Hairy Rove Beetle is one of the most widespread species in its family, and it is found throughout the world, where it has been given many local names. Thankfully, its scientific name seems to have remained relatively stable over time, although some books refer to the species as *Staphylinus maxillosus*.

DEVIL'S COACH HORSE

Staphylinus olens

The Devil's Coach Horse is another sort of rove beetle, as should be apparent from its resemblance to the Hairy Rove Beetle (p. 64). Both are predators, although the Devil's Coach Horse does not visit carrion as much. The Devil's Coach Horse is our largest rove beetle.

Unfortunately, this is one of those bugs with a highly prejudicial English name, which it acquired in England before it was introduced to North America. "Devil's Coach Horse" is an interesting name but a weird one. After all, these beetles don't look anything like horses, and they do not make a habit of pulling things either, the way real coach horses do. Still, the thought of a pair of these beetles pulling a devil and his coach does bring to mind a spooky image. Of course, the devil in question would have to be very, very tiny. A rove beetle the size of a real horse would immediately fall to the ground, unable to get oxygen to its tissues because of its tracheal breathing system—a system that only works if the animal has a bug-sized body.

LENGTH: up to 1.2 in.
HABITAT: open areas.

65

MAY BEETLE

Phyllophaga spp.

The first thing to know about May Beetles is that you don't always see them in May. May is, however, the best month to find them, and they are tough to ignore when you do. These beetles are big, fat, clumsy and stupid. They also fly around at night and are strongly attracted to lights. So, when you are sitting outside on that first warm evening in the spring, you will hear something like "bzzzzh… bzzzahssszzzzzzzzzzzzzzzss…. PFUT! bzt. bzt! Bzzzzzt!… bzzhssssss… bzt." That's the sound of a May Beetle colliding with the porch light, after which the beetle falls on its back and can't find its feet. Kids like these beetles, because you can find them in the morning (if hungry birds don't find them first), and they are fun to play with. They don't bite—once they become beetles, they don't eat. The grubs grow up underground, where they feed on roots for three whole years. On occasion, they are common enough to be real pests. These beetles are members of the grand and glorious scarab beetle family, and they share with other scarabs such features as spiny legs, a sturdy body and many-leaved antennae.

LENGTH: 0.6–0.9 in.
HABITAT: forested areas.

66

TEN-LINED JUNE BEETLE
Polyphylla decemlineata

One of our largest scarab beetles, the Ten-lined June Beetle has awesome antennae, especially on the male. Being many-leaved, the antennae give the impression of a bull moose with seven sets of antlers all stacked up on one another. When a male beetle spreads this magnificent fan to the wind, the scent he seeks is that of the female. These beetles do not live long once they emerge and spend all of their time searching for mates and laying eggs.

In general, the life history of this species is much like that of the May Beetle (p. 66), although the Ten-lined June Beetle quite naturally comes out mainly in July and August. The color pattern of this beetle is also fascinating. If you look closely, with a magnifying glass, you'll see that the stripes on the wing covers are made up of tiny, overlapping scales. The scales are pointed

LENGTH: 1 in.
HABITAT: widespread.

at one end and rounded at the other, and some are white, while the others are tan. They are set in a background of amber-colored cuticle, and each scale is as polished as a piece of hard wax. On the underside of the body, scales mix with long, beige hairs to give the beetle an almost cuddly look.

RAIN BEETLE

Pleocoma spp.

Rain Beetles are another sort of scarab, as you can tell from their antennae. With the first rains of fall, male Rain Beetles appear from the ground and fly around noisily in search of females. This pattern is common for many insects—hot, dry conditions are dangerous, because insects dehydrate easily. A bit of rain brings up the humidity and reduces the threat. Then, the beetles pop out of their pupae and take to the skies. Rain Beetles prefer to fly in the early morning, when conditions are especially cool and moist. However, the females have no wings. Female Rain Beetles live in burrows in the ground, where they patiently wait for the males to find them. The larvae live underground as well, where they feed on the roots of deciduous trees and Douglas-fir.

LENGTH: about 1 in.
HABITAT: forested areas.

Amazingly, a Rain Beetle larva can take up to 13 years to complete its development before pupating. There are many species of Rain Beetles, and biologists have been amazed at how their geographic ranges appear to be both localized and non-overlapping—no one area has more than a single species of Rain Beetle.

GOLDEN JEWEL BEETLE
Buprestis aurulenta

Among people who love beetles, another famous family is the metallic wood-borers. Scientists call them "buprestids," and they are also known as "jewel beetles." Many of these insects are large, iridescent and almost robotic in their movements. They thrive in the heat of summer, and the best place to find them is on the sunlit sides of trees, where they meet their mates and lay the eggs that will become their "flathead-borer" larvae.

One of the finest metallic wood-borers in the Pacific Northwest is the Golden Jewel Beetle. It is widespread, because its larvae live inside dead or dying conifers. The adult beetle is a lovely iridescent green, with shining, orange trim all around the wing covers. Once you learn where to look for them, you'll find jewel beetles in most places that have trees (and even some that don't). The colors of the Golden Jewel Beetle are unmatched by any

LENGTH: 0.7 in.
HABITAT: forests with coniferous trees.

other buprestid species in our area, but this family is worldwide. In the tropics there are big, beautiful species that make ours look puny by comparison. In southeast Asia, many of the most colorful buprestids are often made into real jewelry, set in gold with their legs removed, and sold for a high price.

WESTERN EYED CLICK BEETLE

Alaus melanops

T he Western Eyed Click Beetle is the largest member of the click beetle family in the Pacific Northwest. It is instantly recognizable not only by its size but also by the two eyespots on its pronotum. This beetle lives mostly in rotten wood and under bark, so the eyespots probably serve to startle predators that discover it while searching in these places.

The click beetles are a diverse family, and most of them are confusingly similar in a generally brown and featureless way. Still, they all share the amazing characteristic that gives the family its name—the "click." Turn one over on its back, and it will flail with its legs for a moment or two. Then, it arches its body, and suddenly PUNG!… it flips end over end into the air and, like a tossed coin, lands back on its feet roughly half of the time. The truth is, however, these beetles probably do not click because of this action. In nature, it is doubtful that they fall on their backs on a perfectly flat surface very often. Instead, the click is probably used to startle predators, and some types of click beetles can use the click to launch themselves into the air even before they are upside-down.

LENGTH: about 1.2 in.
HABITAT: dry forests.

MULTICOLORED ASIAN LADYBUG
Harmonia axyridris

Ladybugs eat aphids, and because aphids eat crops and garden plants, ladybugs are generally considered good. Back in the 1920s, entomologists figured that more kinds of ladybugs would mean more goodness, so they brought the Multicolored Asian Ladybug over from Asia, and they released hundreds of them in Washington State, Delaware and Georgia. The Multicolored Asian is now the most common species on both coasts of North America, and it is rapidly colonizing the center of the continent as well. In some places, it has become notorious for its habit of invading buildings by the hundreds of thousands in preparation for winter hibernation. Somehow, no one anticipated this habit when the species was imported to North America.

LENGTH: 0.2 in.
HABITAT: widespread.

To those of us who care about our native ladybugs, the Multicolored Asian is now the bad guy—it seems to outcompete its native relatives. It's hard to be too angry with it, mind you. After all, it is still a ladybug, and among beetles the ladybug is almost everyone's favorite. It's just too bad we think of these beetles as little employees, sent out into the fields to do a job for us by killing our pests. Like us, they are just trying to make a living.

TWO-SPOT LADYBUG

Adalia bipunctata

"There are ladybugs in my house, and it's the middle of winter—what should I do?!" Entomologists hear this concern quite often, and, before the Multicolored Asian (p. 71) arrived, the ladybugs usually turned out to be Two-spots. They get into your house in the fall, looking for a comfy place to hibernate. Then, somewhere in January or February, some of them figure it must be spring, so they start looking for a way out. If you find these misguided beetles on your window panes, you can put them in a cooler place in the house and hope they go back to sleep, or you can offer them a small morsel of liver-flavored cat food as a snack. Apparently, to them it tastes like aphids. Of course, if you have any aphids on your house plants, they prefer them to cat food.

LENGTH: 0.2 in.
HABITAT: trees, shrubs and buildings.

This ladybug is a lovely native species, and it is also amazingly variable. Most have two black spots on a red background, while others have four spots or two red shoulder patches on a black background. After a while, you can recognize these ladybugs across the length of a room, just by their size and shape.

72

CONVERGENT LADYBUG

Hippodamia convergens

The Convergent Ladybug is a native species, and it is common in grassy fields, lawns and gardens. When identifying ladybugs, look at the color, the arrangement and number of spots, the pattern on the pronotum and the overall shape of the beetle. The thing that confuses some people is that a Convergent Ladybug is not just an older, bigger Two-spot Ladybug (p. 72), but instead it is a separate sort of critter, altogether a separate species.

Once ladybugs emerge from the pupae, they don't change their spots, nor do they grow in size. They also don't change their spots to predict weather, as some people once believed. What a strange view of nature! As if one creature exists only to help another one survive—the ultimate in selflessness. Sorry, it just isn't true.

Another myth associated with these ladybugs is that you can buy them for your garden and that they will control your aphids. The ladybugs are collected in their mountain-top hibernation sites, and when you transport them and release them, most simply fly away or go back to sleep. They

LENGTH: 0.3 in.
HABITAT: open areas and hilltops in spring and fall.

congregate while they are hibernating (by the thousands, which makes them easy to harvest), but when they go looking for food, they don't like much company or competition.

CALIFORNIA PRIONUS
Prionus californicus

Who could blame an enthusiastic bugster if one imagined that the California Prionus is the Pacific Northwest's own version of the greatest longhorn beetle of all, *Titanus giganteus*? *Titanus* can be 6 inches long (older books often said it is the size of "a man's hand"), lives in South America and once merited its own article in *National Geographic*. I see nothing wrong with appreciating a bug for its resemblance to a tropical relative. After all, the only thing *Titanus* has that the California Prionus lacks is size, and the Prionus is not a small bug! Both the California Prionus and the tropical *Titanus* are leathery-brown, with big eyes, powerful jaws and a spiked pronotum—all features of their subfamily, the "prionines."

LENGTH: up to 2 in.
HABITAT: western forests.

I first encountered this insect on my birthday, somewhere back in my teens. I was on a family vacation at Parksville, Vancouver Island, lying sick in bed feeling sorry for myself. Then, the biggest beetle I had ever seen flew up and landed on the window screen. I couldn't catch it, but the intensity of that encounter made me forget completely about the flu, and what I had assumed would be a lousy day, with no party and no cake. The appearance of that beetle made sure it was a birthday I would never forget.

PINE SAWYER
Ergates spiculatus

The Pine Sawyer is in most ways very similar to the California Prionus (p. 74). Because they are the two largest beetles in our area, I couldn't resist including them both in this book. Pine Sawyers do indeed grow up in pine trees as larvae, but in truth any conifer will do. Actually, one English name for this species is the "Ponderous Borer." This name is a reference to the fact that they sometimes live in ponderosa pine trees, not that they are "ponderous" in their own right. They do not feed in living trees, only in dead logs and standing snags. Thus, they are part of the fauna that contributes to the formation of forest soil and the turnover of plant matter in the ecosystem. You'd think that would make them economically neutral, along with the rest of the insect decomposers. However, foresters resent the "damage" they do to standing dead trees after a fire, making salvage logging less profitable for them. Bugs just can't seem to win sometimes. According to some sources, this beetle contributed to the origin of a very valuable gift to the logging industry. The beetle's chewing mandibles were the inspiration for the first chainsaw.

LENGTH: up to 2.4 in.
HABITAT: coniferous forests.

75

BANDED ALDER BORER
Rosalia funebris

This species is another longhorn beetle, but it has a very different look from the California Prionus (p. 74) and the Pine Sawyer (p. 75). The longhorn beetles are a very diverse family, and thus systematists have divided it into subfamilies, in which the genera are arranged. Hard-core bugsters learn to recognize the subfamilies of longhorns, along with the subfamilies of scarab beetles and ground beetles. So, the Prionus is a prionine ("PRY-oh-nine"), and the Banded Alder Borer is a cerambycine ("serr-am-BISS-ine").

Many cerambycines have colorful wing covers, and the Banded Alder Borer is one of the nicest. Bugsters sometimes call the whole family "bissids," an abbreviation of the technical term cerambycid ("serr-am-BISS-id").

The larvae of the Banded Alder Borer are wood-borers in deciduous trees, and the adults are often found on or near the trees themselves. They are also attracted to recently painted buildings and sometimes arrive by the hundreds. The antennae of male alder borers are longer than their bodies, while those of the female are shorter. As usual among beetles, however, the female has a heavier body, because she is the one who carries the eggs.

LENGTH: about 1 in.
HABITAT: coastal forests.

BLUE MILKWEED BEETLE

Chrysochus cobaltinus

T his insect is one of those insects that is so darn pretty you really can't walk past it without a second glance. It looks like a great big, carefully polished, shining, bright blue ladybug. Its body is round and plump, and its legs end in what might well be described as paws. In other words, it's a cute beetle and a gorgeous one as well. It is a member of the leaf beetle family, and sure enough, it eats leaves. In particular, the Blue Milkweed Beetle eats the leaves of dogbane and milkweed. These plants produce toxic chemicals to discourage animals from eating them, and the beetle's color is also a warning of its toxicity.

LENGTH: 0.4 in.
HABITAT: open areas.

The beetle will ooze droplets of distasteful liquid when grasped. The beetle's first line of defense, however, is the same as most other leaf beetles—it tucks its legs in and drops to the ground. The Blue Milkweed Beetle is the western equivalent of the Dogbane Beetle (*C. auratus*), and like its eastern cousin, it actually prefers dogbane plants to milkweed. Both species can be found in the Pacific Northwest, but you have to look hard, because they are uncommon.

BLUE HORNTAIL
Sirex cyaneus

Horntails are our largest sawflies, and sawflies are a group unto themselves, on par with bees, wasps and ants. In general, sawflies are pretty inconspicuous insects, but the Blue Horntail gets its share of attention. The adults are big, heavy-bodied and weird-looking, and the females have a pointed ovipositor that makes them look even more fearsome. Fortunately, they are not dangerous, and the ovipositor is not a stinger. Instead, it is used to drill into the wood of trees, where the female lays her eggs, one at a time. The larvae are wood-borers, and some of the horntails are considered pests in some places. When the Blue Horntail gets into lumber, the tunnels of the larvae are conspicuous and difficult to hide.

LENGTH: 1.2 in.
HABITAT: forested areas.

The Blue Horntail is indeed blue—a dark, iridescent blue—but other related species can be banded in yellow and black. These colors give these horntails more of the characteristic look of their order and hint at their relationship to wasps. Perhaps the most unusual aspect of their structure is the fact that they seem roughly cylindrical, with all the main body parts about the same diameter, quite unlike the narrow-waisted, pointy-"abdomened" wasps and bees.

STUMP STABBER
Family Ichneumonidae, Subfamily Pimplinae

T alk to foresters about bugs and a few familiar species will come up time and again: metallic wood-boring beetles, long-horned beetles, horn-tails and Stump Stabbers. A big female Stump Stabber can be 3.3 inches long, including its immense ovipositor, and it looks like something that could definitely hurt you. Many people think the Stump Stabber does sting, despite the assurances of entomologists to the contrary.

Stump Stabbers are also called "ichneumons" (pronounced "ick-NEW-monz"). If you find one, follow it. The female Stump Stabber flies from tree trunk to tree trunk, all the while rapidly drumming its antennae while running around on the bark, quite obviously searching for something. Then, she stops. Somehow, she has detected a wood-boring grub, deep beneath her feet.

At this point, she brings her ovipositor to bear, like some sort of strange miniature oil rig. The insect strains to work the tool into the wood, and eventually she finds the larva and forces a slender, very compressible egg down the tube and into the body of her host. There, the egg will hatch, and the Stump Stabber grub will proceed to devour its victim from the inside out, leaving its essential organs to the last.

LENGTH: with ovipositor, up to 3.3 in.
HABITAT: forests.

COW KILLER

Dasymutilla coccineohirta

The Cow Killer is a member of a group of bugs called "velvet ants." It is not, however, an ant at all. In fact, the familiar wingless, furry Cow Killer is really a female wasp, in the Family Mutillidae. The male looks more like a traditional wasp, and it is smaller and less impressive than the female.

Cow Killers got their name from their sting, and they have some of the most painful stings in the entire insect world. Their bright colors are a warning to potential enemies to avoid them. Cow Killers do not use their stings to kill or paralyze other bugs—instead, they look for the nests of digging wasps and bees and lay their eggs on the prey that the wasps and bees have gathered. Then, the Cow Killer grub eats both the wasp grub and the paralyzed prey intended for the digger wasp.

LENGTH: about 0.6 in.
HABITAT: open, dry ground.

Cow Killers and velvet ants, in general, are omnivores as adults, and they can live for many months as well. Because they are some of the hardiest bugs around, as well as some of the best looking, they are often exhibited in bug zoos, where they make a very interesting display.

FOREST SPIDER WASP

Prionocnemus oregona

Spider wasps resemble thread-waisted wasps in both form and habits, but they specialize in paralyzing spiders. In fact, they form a separate but related family within the overall category of "hunting wasps." Usually, they are at least partially black in color, and many of them have shiny, iridescent blue-black wings.

The most famous member of the family is the giant Tarantula Hawk (*Pepsis* spp.) that lives in the deserts of the American Southwest. Naturalists have long been fascinated by the way this huge, fearless wasp searches out a tarantula spider many times its own body weight, and then deftly avoids the spider's great terrible fangs while maneuvering into position to deliver

LENGTH: about 0.6 in.
HABITAT: open, bare areas in or near forests.

a paralyzing sting. After that, the story is much the same as for most other hunting wasps, complete with a burrow in the ground and a single egg. For the Forest Spider Wasp, the same thing happens, but the wasps are so small that no one notices them, and the spiders that fall prey to their macabre rituals are less imposing than a huge tarantula, at least to us. Still, if you get the chance to watch them, any of the hunting wasps can provide hours of good bug-watching entertainment.

THREAD-WAISTED WASP

Ammophila spp.

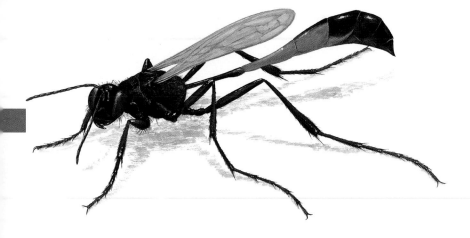

Most wasps are solitary, not colonial. The Thread-waisted Wasp is a member of the digger wasp family, and it has fascinating habits. The female sometimes takes nectar from flowers, but for the most part she spends her days looking for caterpillars. With amazing agility, she stings the caterpillar in the nerve cord and injects a paralyzing poison. The caterpillar is then immobilized but still alive.

With immense power and determination, the wasp then carries the caterpillar back to a burrow that she prepared some time before. She opens the burrow, drags the caterpillar down into the dark, and lays an egg on it. Then she comes back to the surface and closes the entrance, sometimes smoothing it over with a pebble held in her jaws. She then goes off to look for another caterpillar or to dig another burrow. Meanwhile, the egg hatches, and the wasp grub devours the body of the zombie caterpillar. That is, unless some other insect, such as a velvet ant or a parasitic fly, gets its egg into the burrow before it is closed. Then, the invader kills the baby wasp and eats the caterpillar itself.

LENGTH: up to 1.2 in.
HABITAT: open, bare areas.

82

GOLDEN PAPER WASP
Polistes fuscatus

The name "Paper Wasp" really should go to Yellow Jackets (p. 84) and their relatives. By comparison, the "real" paper wasp is an amateur. Paper wasp nests are constructed beneath an overhang of some sort (often the eave of a house), and they have no outside covering. The single layer of paper cells is open to the air, and these wasps never build a second or a third layer. Still, it is interesting to watch paper wasps at the nest, because you can actually see what they are doing—something that can't be said of Yellow Jackets or Bald-faced Hornets (*Vespula maculata*). The colonies of paper wasps are of moderate size, to match the moderate size of their nests. These wasps feed at flowers, especially goldenrod, and they also hunt insects for food. They have painful stings, but our local species is not a particularly defensive one, so few people get stung despite how common the wasps are.

LENGTH: about 0.7 in.
HABITAT: open areas.

To most people, this species is what a "wasp" should look like—long and slender, with a tiny "waist" and narrow wings. To discover that thousands of other insects are called wasps, many of which are tiny and compact, and most of which are not even social, is a surprise to most newcomers to entomology.

YELLOW JACKET

Vespula spp.

I f they didn't sting so much, these wasps would be some of our most watchable bugs. They live in colonies, like Honey Bees (*Apis mellifera*), and they build huge paper nests, sometimes high in the branches of trees, sometimes in old rodent burrows in the ground.

To make paper, Yellow Jackets chew on bark or wood and mix the pulp with saliva. They add each mouthful to the nest, to form either six-sided cells where the larvae are reared or the multi-layered outside cover of the nest. Because each load of pulp comes from a different source, you can see a subtle pattern of gray bands in the paper of the nest. If Yellow Jackets are coming to your fence or lawn furniture for pulp, you will soon notice a series of shallow grooves where they have chewed. For food, they visit flowers, catch bugs and are also attracted to fallen fruit and dead meat.

LENGTH: about 0.4–0.6 in.
HABITAT: widespread.

By the time late summer rolls around, the nests are as big as basketballs, and the hornets are ready to defend them at the slightest provocation. In the fall, the colony breaks down, and only the new queens survive the winter, to start new colonies in the spring. The nests don't last long once the leaves fall—birds pick them apart. Yellow Jackets, unlike Honey Bees, can sting repeatedly, although they do eventually run out of venom, I suppose.

BUMBLE BEE

Bombus spp.

Bumble Bees have a painful sting, but they are so cute and fuzzy that we love them just the same. They are slow to anger and quite docile even when you are near their nest. In the spring, queens set up new colonies in the abandoned burrows of mice and voles. There, they make wax pots, with open tops. Inside these pots, they rear their grubs. Once the grubs grow up to be worker bees, the number of pots increases, and some pots are used to rear the young while others are filled with pollen or honey.

Bumble Bees visit flowers to gather both pollen and nectar. Their wings are so small for the size of their bodies that some biologists were unsure for a while how they could possibly fly. Because they are so hairy, Bumble Bee bodies look bigger than they are. The hair helps hold body heat when

LENGTH: usually 0.4–0.9 in.
HABITAT: clearings and meadows.

they fly, so they can fly at lower temperatures than many other bees. One friend of mine claims that when Bumble Bees come out in the spring, so do the bears, and when the bees go in for the winter, the bears do, too.

CARPENTER ANT

Camponotus spp.

C arpenter Ants are not termites, and termites are not "white ants." They are both social insects, but ants have a pupal stage while termites do not. As well, all worker ants are adult females, while worker termites come in all ages and both sexes. Carpenter Ants are the biggest ants in our area, and they are slow moving and not particularly aggressive. They have no sting, and like many related sorts of ants, their main defense is to bite. Their jaws are strong, because they chew through wood for a living, and that is where they are similar to termites.

In the wild, you can spot a Carpenter Ant nest in a tree trunk by the pile of sawdust outside the entrance. These ants sometimes build their home inside the woodwork of older houses, and there again the thing to watch for is sawdust. They don't actually eat the wood, but in the course of excavating their galleries, they certainly do weaken it, to the point where the tree, or the expensive house, might "fail," as the engineers say. Woodpeckers love to eat these ants, and it is fitting that our biggest ant is continually under attack from our biggest woodpecker, the pileated woodpecker.

LENGTH: about 0.5 in.
HABITAT: forested areas.

HARVESTER ANT

Pogonomyrmex spp.

Harvester Ants make ant hills, and although they don't make the biggest of ant hills, they do make the most obvious ones. In dry country, the mounds of Harvester Ants stand out because the ants prevent plants from growing on or around them. The mound of pebbles keeps the ant colony warm, because it warms up quickly in the sun (the ants also cut down any nearby plants that might shade it). The pebbles are brought up from underground, and it seems that the ants prefer pebbly soil in which to make their colonies. In some places, pale-ontologists search in the Harvesters' pebble pile for tiny fossil teeth. The ants bring any rock-like object to the surface, and, in so doing, they make the paleontologist's job a lot easier. In Montana, Harvester Ants discovered the first-known fossil of the world's oldest primate mammal, *Purgatorius*. Harvester Ants do, indeed, harvest the seeds of grasses and other plants, and they take them to underground chambers where they save them for a rainy day.

LENGTH: about 0.2 in.
HABITAT: open ground.

GIANT CRANE FLY
Holorusia hespera

"Aaaaaaggh! A monster mosquito!" That's what most people say the first time they see a Giant Crane Fly, an event that usually occurs while the fly is resting on the side of a suburban house. There are many species of crane flies, but the giant ones are extra large and have a menacing-looking snout. These flies look evil, but the truth is you couldn't ask for a nicer bug: they don't bite at all, they are actually sort of attractive, and even the larvae are unobtrusive, living as scavengers in the soil and in rotting logs. The European Crane Fly (*Tipula paludosa*), however, has larvae that can be pests in lawns in our area.

Some people also call these flies "daddy long-legs," a term that is most often used to refer to harvestmen (p. 145), which are a sort of arachnid. In general then, we are surrounded by confusion with respect to Giant Crane Flies, and hopefully this book will lead the way to dispelling our

LENGTH: up to 1.4 in.
HABITAT: forested areas.

ignorance. Another frequent twist to the finding-one-in-your-garden story is the fact that they are often discovered while mating, end to end. When a mating pair is disturbed, the sight of two sets of wispy, flailing wings, 12 immense dangling legs and two giant "mosquitoes" tugging in opposite directions, makes for a spectacle that is, let's just say, "creepy" to all but the most devoted bugsters among us.

HORSE FLY

Hybomitra spp.

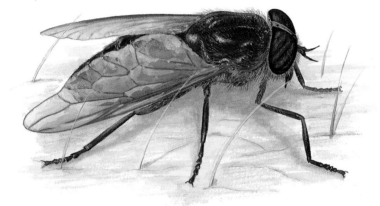

S o what could be interesting about a Horse Fly? Well, how about the colors in its eyes? If you get a close-up look at one—perhaps after a lucky swat—check out the eyes and the intense rainbows that enliven its otherwise evil-looking face. This fly feeds on blood, and it is most common near lakes. Go for a swim in mid-summer, and I guarantee that by the time you have dried yourself off you will have taken at least one swing at a Horse Fly. They are attracted to large mammals (such as ourselves), and the thing they look for is a dark object with a light spot on it where the sun forms a reflective "highlight." If you drive a black car, or a black van, you will find even more of them when you get back to the parking lot.

LENGTH: about 0.6 in.
HABITAT: open areas near water.

One good thing about Horse Flies is that they are so big it's hard for one to bite without you knowing it is there. As well, Horse Flies have large blades in their mouthparts, rather than sophisticated slender stylets like a mosquito. A smaller version of a Horse Fly, with dark markings on its wings, is called a Deer Fly (*Chrysops* spp.). Mind you, Horse Flies will bite deer, Deer Flies will bite horses, and either one will bite people, any chance they get.

BEEISH ROBBER FLY

Laphria spp.

R obber flies don't really steal things, other than life itself. They are amazingly agile predators, and they kill by catching other insects in mid-air. Between hunts, they find a perch on the ground or on vegetation, and from there they scan for potential victims. With large compound eyes, they have excellent vision and an amazing ability not only to spot their prey but also to follow it through the air in high-speed pursuit. When they catch something, they return to the ground with their fearsome proboscis deep in the tissues of their unlucky prey. They are not too distantly related to Horse Flies (p. 89), and they have similar sorts of mouthparts.

LENGTH: about 0.9 in.
HABITAT: shrubby or forested areas.

Even beetles can fall prey to robber flies, and the flies have perfected the way to kill these heavily armored insects. While the beetle is flying, its wing covers are spread, exposing the soft abdomen underneath. The robber fly sinks its mouthparts into the beetle's soft spot while the two are still in the air. Most robber flies are not mimics, but the Beeish Robber Fly looks so much like a Bumble Bee (p. 85) that it is tough to tell the two apart without a close look.

HOVER FLY

Syrphus spp.

I t is important to learn to recognize Hover Flies—it will improve the quality of your life. Why? Because many of them look like wasps, for protection, and it's good to be able to tell a real wasp from a fake one. Look for long antennae and a cylindrical abdomen—that's a wasp. If instead you see tiny antennae and a flattened abdomen—that's a Hover Fly. (Careful! Some wave their front legs as if they were antennae.) The Hover Fly doesn't sting, and it doesn't bite either. In fact, the main thing that it does is hover. Sometimes, a Hover Fly will appear in the air before you and remain so

LENGTH: about 0.4 in.
HABITAT: openings in forested areas.

absolutely still you'd swear there was a string attached to it. As the fly hovers before you, extend your little finger toward it. With practice, you can get these flies to land on your finger. Real masters of hover-fly catching can then reach up with the other hand, and grab the fly by one of its wings!

The larvae of Hover Flies are interesting, too. Some are predators that feed on aphids, while others live in the muck at the bottom of shallow ponds or in carrion. Hover Flies are also called "Flower Flies" by some entomologists.

DRONE FLY
Eristalsis tenax

The Drone Fly is also a sort of Hover Fly, but instead of mimicking wasps, this species mimics the common Honey Bee. The Honey Bee (*Apis mellifera*) is a fairly dull-colored insect, patterned in browns and black, a fact that seems strange in some ways, because such a hard-stinging insect might seem deserving of better warning colors. Both the Honey Bee and the Drone Fly were introduced from Europe. Because the Drone Fly has larger eyes than a female (worker) Honey Bee, it was named for the male (drone) Honey Bee. The larva of the Drone Fly is the famous Rat-tailed Maggot. It lives in the muck at the bottom of ponds and breathes through a long siphon that looks a bit like a rat's tail.

In England, there are many people whose hobby is the study of Hover Flies (p. 91), and there they enjoy the luxury of being able to buy color field guides to their local species. Perhaps some day we will reach the same level of sophistication here, but for the moment just recognizing Hover Flies at all is a good thing. It is also important to appreciate how many Hover Flies are involved in the pollination of flowers—they visit blossoms the same way bees do.

LENGTH: about 0.6 in.
HABITAT: widespread in a variety of habitats.

GREEN LACEWING
Chrysopa spp.

Beautiful, smelly and mean—that's how I think of lacewings. These bugs are familiar in the garden, and the adults are truly elegant with their many-veined wings, their delicate lime green bodies and their bulging golden eyes. The scientific name *Chrysopa* means exactly that: "golden eyes." Catch one, however, and you will soon notice a truly weird smell as it twists and turns in your fingers, while you hold it by the wings. The smell is a bit like coffee, but not really.

As for the mean-spirited aspect of their nature, lacewings are predators, and they mostly eat aphids. Thus, they join ladybugs and the larvae of some Hover Flies (p. 91) in a "friends of the gardener" category, although none of them even know what a gardener is. Young lacewings, which are larvae much like those of a ladybug, are also aphid eaters. They are so vicious that the mother lacewing lays each egg on the top of a long, slender stalk, so the first larva to hatch doesn't eat all of its brothers and sisters before they can get out of the egg. As well as the green ones, watch for brown lacewings and even blotchy ones (both in the Family Hemerobiidae), usually early and late in the season.

LENGTH: about 0.4 in.
HABITAT: widespread in shrubs or forests.

93

ANT LION
Family Myrmeleontidae

At first glance, the adult Ant Lion looks much like a dull brown damselfly. Note, however, its long antennae, which are quite different from the tiny antennae of a damselfly. Ant Lion adults are gentle and quite pretty in their own way. We mostly notice them as they fly to lights at night, although you might also flush them from low vegetation when you go for a walk in places where the larvae live.

Ant Lion larvae are the reason this group of bugs got its name (a literal translation of "Myrmeleontidae"). These bugs live in the sand, where they bury themselves almost completely. Then, like living land mines, they wait. Some lie just below the sand surface, in flat places, while others (the more typical Ant Lions) dig conical pits. When an ant or some other small ground-dwelling bug wanders by, the Ant Lion larva flicks sand at it. With luck, this flicking sand will cause the ant to fall into the pit, where the larva grasps it with long mandibles. The mandibles are hollow, and through them the Ant Lion sucks the life blood of its victims.

LENGTH: up to 1.4 in.
HABITAT: open, dry areas with fine sand or silt in which to dig.

SNAKEFLY

Agulla spp.

L ike the lacewings, Snakeflies are members of the insect order Neuroptera. Some scientists place them in their own order, but they are clearly related to the other Neuroptera (as are beetles, oddly enough). The clues we need to unravel these relationships are now, unfortunately, more than 300 million years old, so you'll have to forgive entomologists for their confusion on this matter.

Snakeflies have an elongated head and thorax, and their front end looks a bit like a snake's head, as long as you ignore the six legs and lacy wings that lie behind. Snakeflies are predators on other small bugs, and they are often seen on flowers or on vegetation. They are truly western bugs, and

LENGTH: about 0.5 in.
HABITAT: open, shrubby areas.

in North America none are found east of the Rockies. As well, the Snakeflies, in general, form a group that is found mainly in the north-temperate parts of the globe and is almost completely absent from the tropics. As a West Coast bugster, I hope you take some pride in this nifty creature, which is often completely unfamiliar to your colleagues elsewhere.

95

SNOW SCORPIONFLY

Boreus spp.

Here's a bug that doesn't mind walking around on the cold snow. It is about the size of a mosquito, and it is very dark in color to allow rapid warming by the weak rays of late winter sun. You can easily distinguish the scorpionfly from other insects by its elongate head; the scorpionfly is also able to jump, which clearly sets it apart from any of the creatures you might otherwise think it is. Snow Scorpionflies feed on mosses, a rare food plant among insects in general.

Scorpionflies form a distinct order of insects, and they are most closely related to two-winged flies and fleas. They go through complete metamorphosis, with a pupal stage. They got their name from more typical members of the group, which have an elongate, clasper-tipped abdomen that is carried over the back the way a scorpion carries its sting. Most scorpionflies also have wings, and two species of small, winged scorpionflies are found in our area (one with wingless females). As a group, the scorpionflies are one of the most poorly studied of the insect orders. There appear to be about 500 species worldwide, and like most sorts of bugs they are most diverse in the tropics.

LENGTH: about 0.1 in.
HABITAT: forested areas.

LACE BUG

Corythucha spp.

Lace Bugs are one of those things that you don't notice until you become a true bugster. Because they are small, they generally escape detection, but once you see one under adequate magnification, you'll be amazed at how intricate and elegant they are. After a while, you will come to realize that given the proper equipment, it doesn't really matter how big a bug is—they are all equally intriguing when you get a good look at them. My own first encounter with lace bugs came at about age six, and even then I was eager to accept the intrinsic coolness of a bug that is not among the biggies.

Lace Bugs get their name from their expanded pronotum, head and front wings, which are reinforced by an irregular honeycomb of struts and veins that give a lacy appearance. These flanges are probably used to protect the bugs' legs from the attacks of tiny predators. Lace Bugs are

LENGTH: about 0.1–0.2 in.
HABITAT: forested areas.

members of the sucking bug order, and they use their sucking mouthparts to suck at the juices of plants. Some are pests, and the easiest place to find them is on the undersides of leaves. In winter, the adults often hibernate under loose bark.

ROUGH PLANT BUG
Brochymena spp.

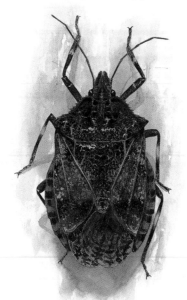

Stink bugs stink, and Rough Plant Bugs are a kind of stink bug. They produce their odor with scent glands, and the smell is unlike anything else that you or I are likely to ever encounter. The smell makes them easy to recognize up close, but these bugs are also obvious in other ways. Stink bugs have broad, pointed shoulders and a large, triangular plate in the middle of their back (the scutellum, for those who like to know these things)—some are more triangular than others, so if in doubt, sniff. Some stink bugs feed on other insects, especially caterpillars, while others suck the juices from plants or plant seeds.

Like Lace Bugs (p. 97), stink bugs are also known for their prowess as devoted mothers. They lay a cluster of intricately sculptured eggs, all together on the surface of a leaf. Then, the mother guards the brood until they hatch, at which point the babies are free to fend for themselves. Baby stink bugs, like all sucking bugs, are much like tiny adults but without wings. The Rough Plant Bug is one of our most abundant stink bugs, and it is a shame that it is not particularly colorful. It is often found under the bark of dead trees in winter.

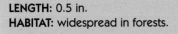

LENGTH: 0.5 in.
HABITAT: widespread in forests.

AMBUSH BUG
Phymata erosa

Small but dangerous, that's an Ambush Bug. It isn't dangerous to people, mind you, but to any sort of insect that visits flowers, it is "trouble in the raw." In the same fashion as a Goldenrod Crab Spider (p. 149), it lies in wait for the unwary pollinators, sometimes tucking in deep among the flower parts so that it stays well hidden. Our Ambush Bug is a yellowish color, with large, angular flanges on the sides of its abdomen. Perhaps these flanges help break up its outline and enhance the ambush effect.

The Ambush Bug has strong middle and hind legs that it uses to hold tight to the flowers. Its front legs, on the other hand, are enormously strong for its size. These legs are the clutches of the Ambush Bug, and with them it can subdue even a gigantic Bumble Bee (p. 85) or a butterfly many times

LENGTH: about 0.4 in.
HABITAT: open areas.

the size of the bug itself. Then, in typical predatory bug fashion, it injects a digestive fluid into its prey, waits for the insides of the insect to soften, and then sucks the insides from its victim. I have seen these insects mainly in the latter part of the summer, when they are easiest to find among the flowers of goldenrod and rabbitbrush plants.

CICADA
Family Cicadidae

In some parts of North America, Cicadas are a big deal, especially when they emerge by the millions, cover the trunks of trees, and drown out all other sounds with their incredibly loud buzzing. The larvae of these big insects live for years underground feeding on roots, and they emerge in early summer. Here in the Pacific Northwest, however, most people don't even know they exist. To find one, you first have to learn what it sounds like: a prolonged, dry, rattling buzz. That's the male, and he sits on a slender branch while singing, often three or more yards above the ground. If you are very stealthy, you might be able to get close enough to spot him. One false move, however, and he will either fly away or go silent.

LENGTH: most about 0.9 in.
HABITAT: dry, forested or shrubby areas.

The sound is produced by a vibrating mechanism in the abdomen, a resonating chamber and a thin membrane something like a banjo skin. For their size, these insects can be incredibly noisy. The Cicada is another sort of bug with a built-in argument, because some people say "SICK-uh-DAHH" or "sih-KAH-duh," while others insist on "sick-AY-dah." All are correct, of course, but I'll let you in on the fact that most entomologists I know say "sick-AY-dah."

ROCK CRAWLER
Family Grylloblattidae

To find these amazing wingless insects, one has to venture either high into the mountains and search among the talus slopes and lava fields, or descend into the moist coastal forests and search among the soft, mossy undergrowth. Some Rock Crawlers also live in caves. The order to which these insects belong was one of the latest to be discovered by science. In 1914 Edmund Walker described the first Rock Crawlers from Banff National Park in Alberta, Canada. He realized that he was looking at not only a new species but also a new genus, a new family and a new order—in other words, a whole new kind of a bug!

To entomologists, Rock Crawlers are interesting because they are so "primitive looking." That means they look like an "average" bug, from which a lot of others could have evolved. To ordinary folks, they have other interesting attributes. For example, if you pick one up and hold it in your hand, the heat from your hulking mammalian body will kill it. That's how well adapted it is to cool climates. An adult Rock Crawler is likely to be seven years old, by the way, and it feeds mainly on other insects, especially wingless crane flies (p. 88).

> **LENGTH:** up to 1.2 in.
> **HABITAT:** cool alpine or forested areas, lava fields and caves.

ROAD DUSTER
Dissosteira carolina

The Road Duster is the signature grasshopper of vacant lots, construction sites, railroad lines and gravel pits. It is often called the "Carolina Locust" or "Carolina Grasshopper." In flight, this remarkable hopper looks like a Mourning Cloak butterfly (p. 37), with black hind wings and a narrow, white border. As a young bug fanatic, I was fooled more than once by this resemblance. Recently, some entomologists have suggested that various band-winged grasshoppers (the subgroup to which the Road Duster belongs) resemble butterflies for a reason. The patterns on some butterflies may advertise to birds that the butterfly is a super-fast flyer, not worth pursuing. Other band-winged grasshoppers resemble sulphur butterflies (p. 31), for the same reason. For Road Dusters, the main defense when in flight is to simply drop to the ground and fold the wings. While on the ground, they are extremely difficult to see, because of their cinnamon brown/gray bodies. They are so much like dirt lumps that even their eyes blend with the color of the rest of the head. Males do an interesting courtship display as well, called the "hover flight." Watch for one to hover in mid-air, about a foot above the ground, fluttering the wings softly, first quickly and then at a slower speed.

LENGTH: 1.2–1.6 in.
HABITAT: open, dry places.

ANGULAR-WINGED KATYDID

Microcentrum rhombifolium

Katydids are wonderful plant mimics. They move slowly, on long, thin legs, and their wings and bodies really do look like green leaves. In the tropics, many katydids are even more leaf-like than ours, with fake bite marks in their wings or fake mold patches. Disguised among the leaves of the trees and shrubs in which they live, katydids carry out their leaf-eating lives.

The males chirp to attract the females, and it is from the sound that one species makes that the name "katy-did" was derived. Bugs called

LENGTH: about 2.4 in.
HABITAT: open areas.

katydids belong to a number of families within a larger group of grigs called "Long-horned Grasshoppers." Indeed, katydids have long antennae, but some members of this gang are also wingless, making them much less like a classic katydid than others. The Angular-winged (or Broad-winged, as it is sometimes called) is one of many Pacific Northwest katydids. It was originally a species of eastern North America, and it has only recently colonized the West Coast.

FIELD CRICKET
Gryllus spp.

There is no more classic sound of summer than the chirping of crickets. Seeing one chirp, on the other hand, is no easy matter. If you do manage to get a peek, you'll find that it is only the males that make sound. Males have two pointy things out the back of the abdomen (the cerci), while females have three (two cerci and one egg-laying ovipositor). To make sound, and hopefully attract females, male crickets rub their two wing covers together, bringing a rasp into contact with a file. The hardened wing covers amplify and resonate to produce the noise we all know and love.

Field Crickets rarely venture into houses. The familiar cricket of the hearth is the House Cricket of Europe (*Acheta domestica*). The House Cricket is brown, while the Field Cricket is black. These days the House Cricket is actually big bug business, because many cricket farms now supply it to pet stores as food for captive frogs, lizards and fishes. It is generally unable to live outdoors year-round in our area, although there are a few such colonies in California.

LENGTH: about 0.9 in.
HABITAT: open areas.

CAVE CRICKET
Ceuthophilus spp.

C ave Crickets, in some places, actually live in caves. Here, however, they mostly live in rodent burrows, under rocks and logs and in rotten wood. What they want is a place that is moist and dark. For those people who think *Homo sapiens* has advanced beyond the "caveman" stage, all I can say is—look in your basement. There, on occasion, you will, indeed, find a Cave Cricket or two. They need access to water, and they are, therefore, usually found some-where near the floor drain. Don't let them worry you, however; they do no harm. Some people mistake them for cockroaches, but I'm assuming that if you are reading this book, you won't do that.

Another name for *Ceuthophilus* Cave Crickets is "camel crickets," based on their hump-backed shape. Note as well that they have no wings, and there-fore they cannot chirp like other crickets. Ours have very long antennae, but the true cave dwellers (in the Pacific Northwest, *Tropidischia xanthostoma*) have even longer feelers, as well as elongate legs. There is a painting of a Cave Cricket in among the famous cave painting of France, some 16,000 years old. It is the oldest depiction of an insect that has ever been discovered. As they say, *plus ça change, plus c'est la même chose*—the more things change, the more they stay the same!

LENGTH: about 0.5 in.
HABITAT: widespread.

PRIMITIVE MONSTER CRICKET

Cyphoderris monstrosa

Whenever I go camping in relatively dry pine forests near the end of the summer, I look for this amazing bug. Males produce a character-istic trilling sound, and they are easy to find with a flashlight after dark, if you are stealthy and patient. Most of the time, they sit on the side of tree trunks, not more than a foot or two above the ground. When you find one, I predict that you will be amazed by its black, white and pink coloration and the ferocious look in its eye.

Some entomologists consider this creature to be a "living fossil." What this expression means is that a once-diverse group of animals, well known in the fossil record, is now represented by only a few living survivors. In a way, I suppose all animals are "living fossils," but let's not get too philo-sophical about that here. Another interesting aspect of the behavior of the Primitive Monster Cricket has to do with courtship. The male's hind wings are replaced by fleshy pads, and he raises his wing covers to allow the female to eat them right off his back—a gift that will probably help her develop healthy eggs as well.

LENGTH: about 1 in.
HABITAT: conifer forests.

JERUSALEM CRICKET

Stenopelmatus fuscus

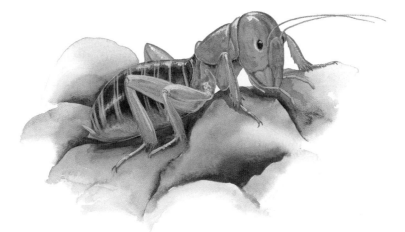

These oddball bugs are in many ways like a "cross between" (actually, I hate that phrase, because almost all examples are biologically impossible, including this one) a Primitive Monster Cricket (p. 106) and a Cave Cricket (p. 105). The Jerusalem Cricket is a big-headed, slow-moving creature that lives most of the time in rocky places along hillsides and canyons. It is a scavenger, and it eats any sort of plant or animal debris that it finds in its nocturnal wanderings.

If you want to see this bug, you might try an old night-bugging trick that I learned from entomologists in Arizona. When you first start out at night with your flashlight and your blacklight, stop by a few rocky places at the bases of hills and place little piles of dry, uncooked oatmeal here and

LENGTH: up to 2 in.
HABITAT: rocky hillsides.

there. Supposedly, Jerusalem Crickets love oatmeal and will slowly make their way toward the pile. Then, when you are packing up your blacklight and getting ready for the drive home, long after midnight, you check the oatmeal. I've been told that you can sometimes find dozens of Jerusalem Crickets this way, but so far all I have seen is ants. The easiest way to find Jerusalem Crickets is to flip rocks and boards during the day.

MINOR GROUND MANTID

Litaneutria minor

Praying mantids (or mantises, if you prefer) are well-known insects. You sometimes see Chinese Mantids (*Tenodera aridifolia*) and Narrow-winged Mantids (*T. angustipennis*) offered for sale in garden shops for control of pests in gardens, but these species are introduced, not native to this area. They also could care less about pest control, but let's not hold that against them. Another introduced species, the European Mantid (*Mantis religiosa*) is found fairly regularly in eastern Washington and Oregon.

Our one and only species of native mantid is the Minor Ground Mantid, and it is certainly an interesting one as well. Minor Ground Mantids live on the ground or in low vegetation, and the females are wingless while the males have wings. These mantids are gray-brown in color and are active during both day and night. Like all other mantids, they can turn their heads to look in any direction they please, and they are lightning-fast predators, catching other bugs in their spiked forelegs. And yes, on occasion, a female will eat her mate during the act of copulation, and he will, indeed, continue mating, even without his brain. Apart from this last unfortunate feature, mantids are surely the most human-like of all bugs.

LENGTH: about 1.2 in.
HABITAT: dry, open areas.

EUROPEAN EARWIG

Forficula auricularia

Very few insects generate the confusion that earwigs do. For reasons that have never been clear, people often believe that they drill into human ears, that they are filthy, and that they can pinch very hard with their cerci. But according to entomologists, who should know, they don't do any of these things. As for how earwigs got their name, your guess is as good as mine. The European Earwig is an introduced species, originally native to Europe, that arrived in North America around 1919. Thus, the name "earwig" is not of local origin.

The truth is that earwigs are interesting, mostly harmless creatures, and that they are also good parents, who guard their eggs and newborn young. Some earwigs are parasitic on other sorts of bugs, while others are omnivores, predators, scavengers or plant feeders. It is the plant-feeding ones that we see most often, including the European Earwig. They especially like to feed on flowers, and this habit naturally angers the gardener who grew the flowers. To my way of thinking, however, flowers grow themselves, and a flower with an earwig in it is infinitely more interesting than one without.

LENGTH: about 0.5 in.
HABITAT: gardens and open areas.

GIANT DAMPWOOD TERMITE

Zootermopsis angusticollis

How lucky can you get? One of the biggest termites on earth lives right here in the Pacific Northwest. Termites are social insects, but, unlike ants, bees and wasps, they do not go through a pupal stage. So, young termites look much like the adults and serve as workers for the colony. The colony is made up of both males and females, again unlike ants, bees and wasps, in which all the workers are female. When they mature, termites can be workers, soldiers or winged "reproductives."

Giant Dampwood Termite workers are about less than an inch long, but a big soldier can be up to 1 inch long, with strong jaws—a very impressive bug. But unless you dig into rotting logs, the termites you are most likely to encounter are the winged ones when they are on late summer flights to find a mate and attempt to start a new colony. Once the queen settles into the job of egg laying, she becomes bloated and helpless and is cared for by workers for her 20 or more years of life.

LENGTH: soldiers up to 1 in.
HABITAT: coastal forests.

Termites eat wood, as anyone knows who lives in a wooden house, but they can't do it without some help. Approximately one third of their body weight is made up of microscopic protozoans. These "gut symbionts" digest cellulose in the wood.

GERMAN COCKROACH
Blatta germanica

It is unfortunate for the German people that this cockroach is named in their country's honor. It is also unfortunate for the many thousands of harmless woodland cockroaches, living in the tropics around the world, that we temperate folks get such a poor introduction to their diversity and splendor. Of course, most of the cockroaches we find in this part of the world are introduced species, and all of these introduced roaches are capable of "infesting" houses and other buildings. There is, however, a native species of large, colonial wood roach (*Cryptocercus punctulatus*) in southeastern Oregon.

Cockroaches seem especially to like greenhouses. Once under a safe roof, they feed on just about anything edible, although they do need water, which they get from condensation or from water traps and drain-pipes. They are active after dark and very difficult to catch. Their cerci (the two feelers on the end of the abdomen) can detect even the slightest breezes, and cockroaches instantly run when they feel the pressure wave of an approaching foot. Cockroaches are very rarely implicated in the spread of disease, despite what you might hear. Generally, they are most abundant in places where things are most messy, and in those sorts of environments diseases have no problem getting around by themselves.

LENGTH: about 0.6 in.
HABITAT: buildings, potentially anywhere in our area.

BOREAL BLUET
Enallagma boreale

I f you have ever spent time beside a pond or a lake in spring or early summer, you have seen these bluer-than-blue bugs. Like phosphorescent toothpicks, they hover among the reeds, where they catch their prey by plucking it off leaves while in flight. Aphids and baby grasshoppers are about the right size for a damselfly to tackle, and yes, Boreal Bluets are a type of damselfly. More specifically, they are a type of American bluet.

The males are patterned in blue and black, while some females are green or yellow, instead of blue. To be honest, our five species of American bluets all look more or less exactly alike. In cases like this one, entomology books usually say something like "identification is best left to specialists." In reality, it's not that hard; all you need is a good magnifying glass and some obscure information. More and more, however, the popularity of damselfly- and dragonfly-watching is catching up to butterfly-watching, which in turn is slowly catching up to bird-watching. If you've tried bird-watching, and if you believe that mere mortals can actually identify sparrows and shorebirds in the field, then you might some day agree that the bluets are manageable, too.

LENGTH: about 1.2 in.
HABITAT: ponds and lakes.

COMMON SPREADWING
Lestes disjunctus

These damselflies have only a bit of blue on them, right at the tip of the abdomen and again at the base of the wings. When they are young, they are iridescent green or brown, and as they get older they become covered in a waxy powder, like the "bloom" on a plum. This powder has led damselfly specialists to call it "pruinosity," from the same root as "prune." The spreadwing damselflies are most common later in the summer, when their pruinosity is fully developed.

Together, damselflies and dragonflies form the insect order Odonata, and, unfortunately, we have no English term that refers to them both together. British people use the word "dragonfly" in this way, but it seems to me that giving "dragonfly" two confusingly similar meanings is a bad idea. I prefer the term "odonates" or just simply "odes" myself. Telling damselflies from dragonflies is easy: damselflies are thin, and all of their wings are similar in shape; dragonflies are more heavily built, and the hind wings are broader than the front ones. Some people will tell you that damselflies always fold their wings over their backs, but obviously the spreadwings are an exception to this rule.

LENGTH: 1.4 in.
HABITAT: ponds and lakes.

BLUE-EYED DARNER

Aeshna multicolor

T he darners are our biggest dragonflies, and the Blue-eyed Darner is one of the most common of the darners. Up close, the male is a dark brown insect, patterned in blue and green, usually with beautiful blue-green and black-spotted eyes. Some of the females are colored this way, while others are brown and yellow. Darners spend most of the day on the wing, cruising the mid-summer skies for insects, which they capture in flight with their long, spiny legs. Darners breed in ponds and lakes, but they will also wander far from water to feed.

The name "darner," by the way, comes from the mistaken notion that these dragonflies will sew up your lips with their stinger. In reality, they have no stinger, and they don't sew, so put aside your fears. Some entomologists have suggested that this rumor got started when people wading in the shallows were accidentally jabbed by female darners, which were trying to lay eggs. I guess a bare leg is easy to mistake for a soft water plant. Darners are on the wing from late spring all the way to late fall.

LENGTH: 2.8 in.
HABITAT: widespread.

GREEN DARNER
Anax junius

The Green Darner is not only big and beautiful, it is also a migrant. Each spring, Green Darners move northward with the warm weather, usually ensuring that they are the first large dragonflies to appear on the wing in any given location. They then breed in ponds and shallow lakes, and their progeny apparently hatch out before the fall and stage a return migration south. Perhaps it is this migrating tendency that has made Green Darners the most common and widespread large dragonflies in North America. This species is also found in Hawaii, alongside its gigantic relative the Hawaiian Darner (*A. strenuus*).

A male Green Darner is actually only green on the thorax—the abdomen is bright blue. In fact, the blue base of the male's abdomen

LENGTH: up to 3.1 in.
HABITAT: near ponds and lakes.

is a good field mark, making this species easily recognizable at a distance. The female, on the other hand, is much more greenish looking, although her abdomen is actually grayish or brownish.

PALE SNAKETAIL

Ophiogompus severus

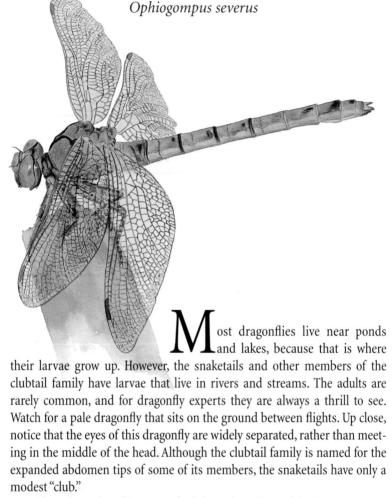

Most dragonflies live near ponds and lakes, because that is where their larvae grow up. However, the snaketails and other members of the clubtail family have larvae that live in rivers and streams. The adults are rarely common, and for dragonfly experts they are always a thrill to see. Watch for a pale dragonfly that sits on the ground between flights. Up close, notice that the eyes of this dragonfly are widely separated, rather than meeting in the middle of the head. Although the clubtail family is named for the expanded abdomen tips of some of its members, the snaketails have only a modest "club."

The Pale Snaketail is easy to find along the valleys of the bigger rivers in mid-summer. Notice that their coloration includes none of the intense blues and reds of other dragonflies. Instead, they are a light "grass" green. Green color in animals is typically produced by a combination of yellow pigment and a blue "scattering" of light—the same thing that makes the sky blue. In other words, "Why is the sky blue?" is a much simpler question than "Why is the snaketail green?"

LENGTH: 2 in.
HABITAT: widely distributed along streams and rivers.

116

AMERICAN EMERALD
Cordulia shurtleffi

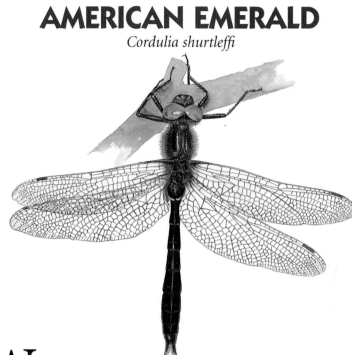

What a fine dragonfly this is! With gleaming green eyes and a jade black, iridescent body, it has a certain style all its own. The American Emerald is our most common member of the emerald family. It is a species of early summer, and it lays its eggs in ponds and small lakes, which is probably why it is so common. Other sorts of emeralds prefer boggy pools deep in black spruce and tamarack peatlands or high mountain lakes, and this habitat contributes not only to their rarity but also to their appeal.

To get a good look at any of the emeralds, it really does help to catch them. The "odonatist" waits, crouching by a skinny little brook, as it flows

LENGTH: 1.8 in.
HABITAT: widely distributed in ponds and lakes.

through the shaded woods. Mosquitoes swarm by the dozens, but the stalker dares not swat them for fear of spooking a passing dragonfly. When one finally comes in reach, one swing of the net is all it will allow, and with it you either bag the emerald or you do not.

It's hard to say whether emeralds or clubtails (p. 116) generate more excitement among dragonfly enthusiasts, but it's probably safe to say that the clubtails rule in the south, while the emeralds are symbols of the great northern forests.

WESTERN PONDHAWK
Erythemis collocata

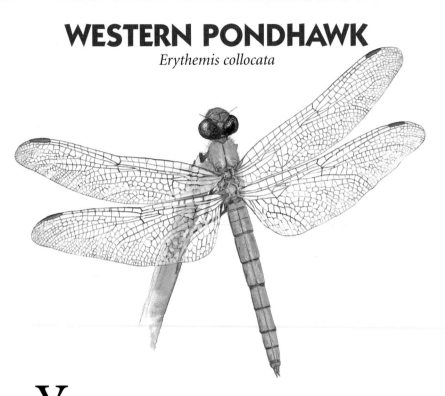

Y ou must admit "Western Pondhawk" is a great name. It was arrived at in a highly democratic fashion. The Dragonfly Society of the Americas called for nominations, the nominations were placed on a ballot, and all the members were allowed to vote. This group of animals is, to my knowledge, the only group in North America that got its English names in this fashion. In most other cases, a committee was formed and then delivered its list of approved names from on high.

The Western Pondhawk is a good-looking, bright green or blue dragonfly that lives near ponds and lakes. Young males are green, but as they age their pruinosity (see p. 113) turns them blue. The Western Pondhawk often rests on bare ground or wood, and it is, therefore, easy to mistake for a snaketail. In Eastern North America, the very similar Eastern Pondhawk (*E. simplicollis*) is more inclined to perch in foliage. In older books on dragonflies, the two species are confused, and it took specialists some time to figure out that there are two separate species involved and not just one widespread species after all.

LENGTH: about 1.8 in.
HABITAT: bare places near ponds and lakes.

118

COMMON WHITETAIL

Libellula lydia

T o my eye, this dragonfly is one of the prettiest of all. I love to see it patrolling around a small pond, stopping to perch on a low stick here or there, just barely protruding from the water. The broad, bright bluish-white abdomen of a mature male is a wonderfully obvious example of signal coloration. Of course, it uses this beacon to ward off other males and to advertise to females. The color of the abdomen comes from—you guessed it—pruinosity, just as in the Western Pondhawk (p. 118) and the Common Spreadwing (p. 113). Then there are the black-banded wings, contrasting dramatically with the blue-white abdomen. You might think that this sort of color would make the Common Whitetail easy prey for birds, but the truth is that few birds can outmaneuver one of these agile dragonflies in the air. With its stout thorax, short wings and broad body, the Common Whitetail is maneuverable indeed, as you will surely learn if you ever try to net one.

LENGTH: about 1.8 in.
HABITAT: near ponds.

Female Common Whitetails have a brown abdomen with white flecks along the sides, and wings that each have three black bands.

FOUR-SPOTTED SKIMMER

Libellula quadrimaculata

T he name of this fine dragonfly proves one thing beyond any doubt—
entomologists can't count. Because the wings on one side look just like
the wings on the other, I guess they didn't bother looking for all eight black
spots. If you count the black hind wing bases, there are really 10 spots, but at
this point who cares? With a thick, muscular body and a broad, streamlined
abdomen, it is a handsome animal. When it is in the prime of its life, its
colors are vivid orange and black, but they do fade as the dragonfly gets older.

You see the Four-spotted Skimmer mostly around ponds and lakes,
and it seems to like patrolling along the reedy shoreline. Females lay
eggs by themselves, by dipping their
abdomen in the water while they fly.
Males of many other dragonflies
remain attached, so no other male
can interrupt the egg-laying process and mate with the female again. This
species also lives in Europe where it is famous for its mass migrations, which
blacken the skies, or for its coming to rest by the thousands on ocean-going
ships. Too bad these situations don't happen in the Pacific Northwest as well.

LENGTH: about 1.7 in.
HABITAT: near ponds and lakes.

VARIEGATED MEADOWHAWK

Sympetrum corruptum

"Variegated" is a word that means "marked with irregular patches of different colors," but why *corruptum*, which simply means "corrupt?" Some experts think the name refers to the stagnant waters that are sometimes the breeding places for this species of dragonfly. When you are the one up to your armpits in waders, trying to catch dragonflies, it's easy to form strong opinions about smelly habitats.

The Variegated Meadowhawk is another dragonfly that sometimes stages mass migrations. It is a widespread species, but the migrations are often most noticeable right here on the coasts of Washington and Oregon. The migrations occur in the fall, and they seem to be triggered by an east wind. That's when observers report seeing huge waves of Variegated Meadowhawks moving south along the coastline. Where they came from,

LENGTH: about 1.6 in.
HABITAT: usually near ponds and lakes.

and where they are going, no one yet knows! Most of these migrators are immatures, by the way, and are less red than the mature male pictured here.

SNOW FLEA
Family Isotomuridae

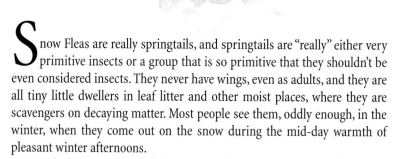

Snow Fleas are really springtails, and springtails are "really" either very primitive insects or a group that is so primitive that they shouldn't be even considered insects. They never have wings, even as adults, and they are all tiny little dwellers in leaf litter and other moist places, where they are scavengers on decaying matter. Most people see them, oddly enough, in the winter, when they come out on the snow during the mid-day warmth of pleasant winter afternoons.

With their amazing "tails," they leap about on the surface of the snow, obviously immune to the cold. The tail is actually an organ that comes out of the bottom of the springtail's abdomen, and it is used like a catapult to fling the bug up into the air. Most likely, these springtails are not entirely pleased to be on the snow and are trying to get to someplace where the snow has melted—so they can go back to life the way they like it. It is possible that they do find things to eat on the snow, however, and if you have a good close look at the surface of partly melted snow you'll see it's not as clean as it looks from up high.

LENGTH: up to 0.08 in.
HABITAT: widely distributed.

STREAM SKATER
Aquarius remigis

L et's face it—it's just plain weird that an animal can live on top of the water without falling through. A Stream Skater achieves this feat in a fascinating way—four very long legs support its slender body, and thus its wispy mass is distributed over a large area of the water's surface. The water itself has a sort of skin to it (the "surface tension") that is strong enough to support an insect, but only if its legs repel water, which naturally a Stream Skater's do. For these little bugs, the surface of a stream must feel like a great, slippery waterbed mattress, stretching off in all directions. On this bizarre playing field, they search for food in the form of other bugs that have fallen in and drowned or that are in the process of drowning.

LENGTH: up to 0.9 in.
HABITAT: streams and small rivers.

Because Stream Skaters are sucking bugs, they have a piercing proboscis that allows them to overpower and consume their prey—mostly bugs that have fallen in the water. Some full-grown Stream Skaters have wings, while some are wingless. Those Stream Skaters that are winged can leave the stream and settle elsewhere, while those that are wingless must be satisfied with their humble home and trust that things will remain to their liking.

GIANT WATER BUG

Lethocerus americanus

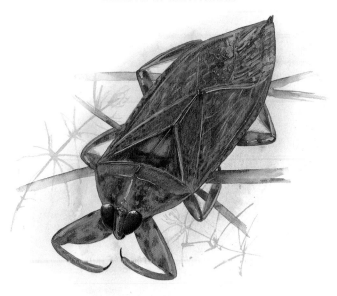

With its swollen front legs, this critter looks a bit like a muscled weightlifter holding two long spikes above his head. Oddly enough, it also looks like a domino-sized piece of wet, brown cardboard. In flight, it looks a lot like a small bat, and it is often attracted to lights at night.

Once a Giant Water Bug grasps a luckless fish, tadpole or fellow insect, the result is inevitable. The sucking beak plunges deep, and digestive juices are injected. Because of these juices, the prey dissolves inside its own body, while the willow leaf–sized insect holds on and waits until the time is right to suck. When the meal is done, the bug swims off to digest, using two pairs of swimming legs, not one. After all, it is our largest aquatic insect, and it needs the extra power to propel its hefty body through the water. Young Giant Water Bugs look much like the adults but without wings. These impressive creatures can be found in still or slow-flowing waters, and they are most abundant in cattail marshes. And yes, if one bites you, it really does hurt.

LENGTH: 2 in.
HABITAT: ponds and lakes.

WATER BOATMAN
Family Corixidae

Although it is small, the Water Boatman is amazing. Take a look at its legs. The first pair are shaped like little garden trowels, and the bug uses them for sifting through muck for food. The next pair are long and pointed, and the boatman uses them to hold onto plants or rocks while underwater. Then, there are the back legs, which are the boatman's oars.

If you keep a Water Boatman in an aquarium, you can see how it breathes underwater. A layer of air clings to the boatman's tummy, and it breathes from this bubble. The oxygen the bug needs enters the bubble from the surrounding water. At the same time, carbon dioxide leaves the bubble and goes into the pond. Slowly, the bubble gets smaller as nitrogen goes into the water, and then the bug pops to the surface to replenish its air supply.

Water Boatmen live in ponds, rivers, lakes and even saline sloughs.

LENGTH: 0.2–0.4 in.
HABITAT: ponds, lakes, rivers and streams.

At times, there can be millions of them in one place, and when they accidentally fly to lights at night, they can cover the ground with their bodies.

SINGLE-BANDED BACKSWIMMER

Notonecta unifasciata

Are you any good at the back-stroke? Well, it seems that the backswimmer doesn't know any other way to swim. At first, you might think that a backswimmer is just an upside-down Water Boatman (p.125) but have another look. Both pairs of front legs are short and stocky, for grabbing prey. Instead of resting on underwater plants, backswimmers lounge right at the top of the pond. They rest with their legs touching the underside of the water surface, and their heads aimed slightly downward, ready to dive.

If you catch one and flip it over, you'll see how pretty it is, with bright white wings and fiery red eyes. Don't let it bite you though! The bite of a backswimmer is like that of a Giant Water Bug (p. 124)—intended to dissolve your flesh! People who keep fish in outdoor ponds dread backswimmers, because they eat a lot of small fishes, as well as other bugs. In nature, however, they are both the predator and the prey, and they make the world of the pond more interesting, even if it is a bit more dangerous. Backswimmers may be predators, but they live in fear of such things as Giant Water Bugs, diving beetles and fishes, too.

LENGTH: 0.4 in.
HABITAT: ponds, lakes and slow streams.

WATER SCORPION
Ranatra sp.

Structurally, a Water Scorpion is built almost exactly like a Giant Water Bug (p. 124) but on a much slimmer plan. To look at these scorpions, however, you'd think you were gazing at an underwater praying mantid. Water Scorpions do, indeed, catch their buggy prey with their forelegs,

> **LENGTH:** up to 1.2 in, not counting the breathing tube.
> **HABITAT:** ponds and lakes.

the way mantids do, but their forelegs are not spiked, and their heads do not turn to look at things all around them. As well, they have piercing, sucking mouthparts, not the chewing mouthparts of mantids (pp. 108–11). Amazingly, they can get up out of the water and fly to a new pond, when the need arises—or at least the adults can. Young Water Scorpions look much like their parents but without wings.

Water Scorpions breathe through a siphon that extends out the back of their abdomens. It is not a tube, but rather it is two parallel rods of cuticle with water-repellent hairs on them. Because the surface tension of the water cannot penetrate the hairs, the siphon acts like a tube even though it is not solid.

WHIRLIGIG BEETLE

Gyrinus spp.

This water beetle is probably the coolest of all. With the most efficient swimming legs in the entire animal world, it zips around on top of the water spinning and whirling like a super-fast bumper car. If it needs to, it can dive underwater and swim with the fishes, and it also has wings when the time comes to find a new pond. Sometimes, dozens of them band together to form a frenetic flotilla on the surface.

If you have a microscope, and a whirligig specimen, you can see how amazing its eyes are. Each eye is actually split in two! One half looks up into the air, while the other half watches down into the water. Of course, while this water beetle is spinning and whirling at high speed its eyes need all the help they can get, so the water beetle also uses its short, triangular antennae to "feel" its way through the twists and turns.

LENGTH: about 0.2 in.
HABITAT: ponds, lakes and streams.

Whirligig Beetles are predators, and they will eat any unfortunate bug they can catch on the water's surface. Even baby water striders are not fast enough to get away from them. And if another animal tries to eat a whirligig, it gets a mouthful of something that smells a lot like rotting fruit.

POLISHED DIVING BEETLE

Agabus spp.

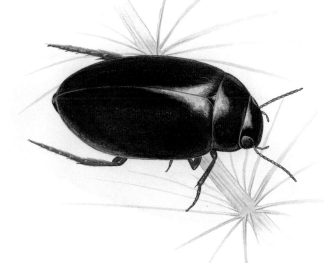

You mostly find these beetles in natural ponds, rather than in the sorts of meltwater ponds that form in parks and schoolyards in the spring. They are not rare, but they are always exciting to catch. Polished Diving Beetles are usually pure black or brown, with strongly arched backs. You might not think that this shape would be the most hydrodynamic one for a beetle, but then these beetles don't do much fast open-water swimming. They are usually found in among dense clots of water plants, or prowling through the debris on the bottom of shallow waterbodies.

There are 82 species of Polished Diving Beetles in the U.S., and each has its own preferred habitat. Some of them live in permanent ponds, some in temporary ponds and some in flowing water. Some species spend the winter as eggs, some as larvae and some as adults. In England, one species of Polished Diving Beetle lives only in bogs, and as the bogs of England became increasingly degraded, the beetle became increasingly rare—a small but typical lesson in the importance of conserving biodiversity and in paying attention to bugs.

LENGTH: about 0.2–0.4 in.
HABITAT: ponds, lakes and slow streams.

129

GIANT DIVING BEETLES
Dytiscus marginicollis

Next to the Giant Water Bug, and some really big Dragonfly Larvae, these are our biggest aquatic insects. They, too, are powerful predators that will eat almost anything they can overpower. If you keep pond critters in an aquarium, you will find that sooner or later there is only one left, and in most cases the survivor will be either a Giant Water Bug (p. 124) or a Giant Diving Beetle. The most impressive member of this group of beetles is the Harris's Diving Beetle (*D. harrisii*), and a big one can be 1.6 inches long!

Female Giant Diving Beetles come in two forms, in most species. The first form looks a lot like the male, with shiny black wing covers. The second form has grooves running the length of the wing covers, making it look at first glance like it must be a different species. A female with a white blob on the end of her abdomen has been mated—the white stuff discourages other males from mating with her again. Males have round sucker pads on their front feet, for holding onto the slippery females. If you notice a bad smell when handling these beetles, it is probably their defense chemicals. These steroids are powerful, and predators respect them.

LENGTH: 1 in.
HABITAT: almost any freshwater, usually not flowing.

WATER SCAVENGER BEETLE

Hydrophilus triangularis

Here we have a water beetle that is not a ferocious predator. Water scavengers are the gentle ones in the water beetle crowd (the adults, that is—larvae are ferocious predators), and they feed on plants and on various sorts of debris. When they swim, they paddle like crazy with all six legs, and most of the time they cling to underwater plants. In many ways, they look like they are trying to pretend they are not underwater at all, like leaf beetles on the willows by the shore.

Whereas the diving beetles (pp. 129–30) keep their air supply under their wings, hidden from view, the water scavengers keep air both under the wings and all along their undersides. Underwater, they look like they are coated with liquid mercury. To replenish the bubble, they don't just bob to the surface either. Instead, they barely stick their head up, and let the air flow in around their antennae. For water scavengers, life is careful and slow. For diving beetles, it is risky and fast. This species (*H. triangularis*) is the biggest Water Scavenger Beetle in North America. Smaller types abound, mind you, and the large ones are certainly not typical of their family.

LENGTH: 1.4 in.
HABITAT: ponds and lakes.

131

SALMONFLY

Pteronarcys californica

Salmonflies are also called "Giant Stoneflies," because they are our largest member of the stonefly group. Salmonflies are encountered frequently by people walking near rivers. When they least expect it, there is suddenly a huge, flattened insect crawling on their clothes in a frenzied and highly unnerving manner. Of course, like most bugs, they can't harm you, and they don't want to harm you. Still, most people would prefer to be introduced to stoneflies another way.

Another way that many people get to know this group is by reading dinosaur books. When you look at paintings of amphibians and reptiles that "ruled the earth" before the dinosaurs, there are often stoneflies added by the artist, along with other ancient sorts of bugs, such as dragonflies and cockroaches. Leaving aside the fact that we all know that bugs, not dinosaurs, have always ruled the earth, it is interesting that Salmonflies have remained more or less unchanged for about 300 million years. They are also interesting to watch in the here and now, especially when they drum their abdomens on the stems of plants, as a courtship signal to the opposite sex. In flight, however, they are a far cry from masters of the air, proving that for almost a third of a billion years, it really didn't matter.

LENGTH: 1.6 in, including the folded wings.
HABITAT: common along rivers and streams.

132

MAYFLY LARVA
Order Ephemeroptera

Some kinds of bugs seem to exist only for the sake of getting eaten by other creatures, which, of course, isn't true, although it sure seems that way. Mayflies and their larvae are one such group, and they are about as defenseless as a bug can get. The adults don't even feed.

The one pictured here is part of a group of Mayfly Larvae called "crawlers." The other 100–200 species of mayflies in this part of the world are either crawlers, burrowers or swimmers. Each one has its own style of feeding, and they all eat things like algae and detritus. Some of them even sieve food from the water, with their hairy front feet. Some Mayfly

LENGTH: up to 1.2 in.
HABITAT: freshwater, mainly rivers and streams.

Larvae live in streams, some in ponds, some in lakes and some in rivers. The easiest way to recognize them is by their three-pronged abdomen tip and the fuzzy gills that line the sides of their abdomen.

When mayflies emerge as adults, they generally live only a single day. At first they are called "duns" or "subimagos"—an odd stage that no other insect goes through. Next, they shed their skin again, wings and all, and become the short-lived true adult that lives only long enough to mate and lay eggs.

133

DAMSELFLY LARVA

Order Odonata, Suborder Zygoptera

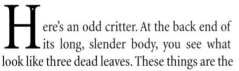

Here's an odd critter. At the back end of its long, slender body, you see what look like three dead leaves. These things are the insect's gills, with which it takes oxygen from the water. Six long legs help it scramble among the underwater plants, where it watches for prey with its bulging compound eyes. When a small, edible insect is spotted, the larva takes aim and… schnik! The folded lower lip shoots out, many times the length of the larva's head, and grabs the unlucky prey like the tongue of a chameleon lizard.

Damselfly Larvae are common in ponds and lakes, and they are easy to recognize. They are not good swimmers, mind you, and when they do have to swim, they wiggle through the water like a person with their hands at their sides. If you look closely at the top of a Damselfly Larva's thorax, you'll see four little wing pads. These wing pads will eventually become the adult damselfly's wings, when the larva finally climbs up out of the water and sheds its skin for the final time.

LENGTH: up to 1.1 in.
HABITAT: ponds, lakes and streams.

DRAGONFLY LARVA
Order Odonata, Suborder Anisoptera

D amselfly Larvae are weird, but Dragonfly Larvae are even weirder. Both have the folding lower lip that catches prey, and both have big eyes and slender legs, but there the similarities seem to end. Dragonfly Larvae are bigger, heavier and more powerful that Damselfly Larvae (p. 134). As well, instead of leaf-like gills, the Dragonfly Larvae keep their gills inside the end of their abdomen, in their rectum. That means, I'm afraid, that they breathe with their butt. And when they need to swim, what do they do? They squirt water out their back end and shoot through the pond with jet propulsion.

The larvae of the darner dragonflies are long and streamlined, like the one shown here. Skimmer Dragonfly Larvae have longer legs and fatter bodies, sometimes with lots of spikes out the sides. Often, they become covered with algae and pond "gunk." Perhaps the oddest dragonfly larvae are the clubtails that spend their lives partly buried in mud at the bottom of streams and rivers and have smaller eyes and shorter legs. No matter what the species, Dragonfly Larvae take at least a few months to grow up, and when they emerge to become adults, they crawl up on plants or on the sandy banks of rivers.

LENGTH: up to 1.9 in.
HABITAT: ponds, lakes and streams.

135

CADDISFLY LARVA
Order Trichoptera

To most people, an adult caddisfly doesn't quite qualify as a "cool" bug. It is moth-like and only moderately colorful, and the only obvious things that set it apart from other bugs are its wispy, long antennae. But every caddisfly was once a larva, and Caddisfly Larvae are just plain nifty. Most Caddisfly Larvae are scavengers, but some eat algae, which they graze from rocks and water plants, while others are predators. When they are getting food, they are constantly at risk from all of the underwater predators around them. So these larvae protect themselves with cases—coverings for their soft, grublike bodies. Some of these larvae make the cases from twigs, while others use pebbles, reeds or leaves, held together with silk and saliva. Most cases are straight, but some are coiled like a snail shell.

LENGTH: up to 2.4 in.
HABITAT: ponds and lakes.

To find Caddisfly Larvae, look into a shallow pond, and watch the bottom. Pretty soon, you'll see things move that you thought were just debris. They are the larva cases. Trout eat many of these insects, by the way, and experiments have shown that they recognize Caddisfly Larvae by looking for their eyes. "If it has eyes, it must be alive" is the trout's rule, and when you think of it, that's not a bad way to find bugs yourself.

WATER TIGER

Dytiscus spp.

The Water Tiger is really just
the larva of the Giant Diving Beetle (p. 130).
Other sorts of diving beetles have similar larvae, too.
The name "Water Tiger" leads some people to confuse the diving beetles and
the tiger beetles, but tiger beetles only live on land and never in the water,
at least in this part of the world.

A Water Tiger is a marvelous beast. It swims with all six legs, in a very
graceful fashion, floating almost effortlessly through the pond. On its broad,
flat head the Water Tiger has eyes, but
they are simple eyes, not the large
compound eyes of the adult. As well,
whereas the adult kills its prey by
chewing on it with short but powerful jaws, the jaws of the Water Tiger are
like two hypodermic needles. The Water Tiger swims up to its prey, and then
attacks quickly and savagely. Once a fish or tadpole has been impaled, digestive juices are injected, and the prey dissolves in its own body. You might
think this method of killing would make Water Tigers some of the most fearsome creatures in the pond, but they often fall prey to both Giant Water Bugs
(p. 124) and the adults of their own species. Most Water Tigers prefer to eat
small vertebrates, but some are more fond of eating insects instead. Like the
adults, Water Tigers have to come to the surface to breathe, and their breathing hole is located right at the tip of their abdomen.

LENGTH: up to 2.4 in.
HABITAT: ponds and lakes.

SALMONFLY LARVA

Pteronarcys spp.

At first the larva of a Salmonfly might look a lot like a great big Mayfly Larva (p. 133), but look closely and notice the differences. Salmonflies are a type of stonefly, and stoneflies form an insect order separate from the Mayflies. A Stonefly Larva has only two long feelers on the end of its abdomen, where a Mayfly usually has three. The Stonefly Larva will keep this feature as an adult, and, in fact, an adult stonefly looks a whole lot like a larva, except with wings. When the biggest of our stoneflies emerge as adults, fishermen call them "Salmonflies" and trout go wild trying to eat as many as possible while the feast lasts.

LENGTH: up to 2 in.
HABITAT: rivers and streams.

Stoneflies don't live in ponds or lakes—they only like streams and rivers. Even then, they seem to prefer clear, fast-flowing water, with lots of dissolved oxygen. Unlike Mayfly Larvae, with gills on the sides of their abdomens, Stonefly Larvae gills are tucked into their leg pits, so to speak. Without a powerful magnifying glass, and an upside-down larva, they are tough to see.

What do Stonefly Larvae eat? Mostly water plants and algae, much like Caddisfly Larvae and Water Scavenger Beetles (p. 131), but some are predators. With their powerful legs, they hold onto underwater rocks and fight the current that threatens to sweep them away.

SOW BUG
Oniscus aselus

In general, insects are the bugs of the land, while crustaceans are the bugs of the sea. Some crustaceans, however, do live on land, although they need moist places to survive, because they breathe with modified gills. Remember, crabs are also crustaceans, and we have all seen the air-breathing hermit crabs that are such popular critters in pet stores. Even sea-shore crabs can spend a fair amount of time out of the water, up on rocks or sand.

Sow Bugs were accidentally introduced from—where else?—Europe. It is interesting that European bugs generally do well when they are introduced to North America, but in reverse it doesn't work the same way. Sow Bugs are sometimes confused with Pill Bugs (*Armadillidium vulgare*—also a European import), but Pill Bugs roll up into a ball when they are frightened, and Sow Bugs do not. They are both slow-moving, heavily armored creatures that are easily recognized by their many legs and their many-segmented shell of a body. They are not harmful, and they feed only on decaying material, both plant and animal. Because our gardens are almost completely unnatural ecosystems to begin with, the addition of Sow Bugs is not much different from adding another species of non-native flowering plant.

LENGTH: about 0.4 in.
HABITAT: gardens and disturbed areas.

GARDEN CENTIPEDE

Lithobius sp.

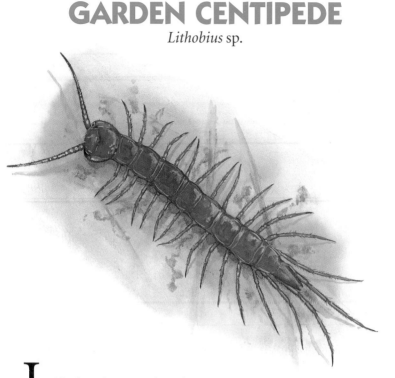

Lift a board, or turn the soil in your average garden, and you're likely to find a centipede. The typical specimen is about 1 inch long and rusty orange in color. It moves rapidly, twists like a miniature snake and can squeeze into what seem like the tiniest openings to escape—probably why you also find them in basements so often. A slight opening between a window and the foundation or a crack between wood and cement will allow them to get in. Once in the house, however, they are no longer in contact with their most cherished substance—moisture. They quickly dry out indoors, and usually when you find them, they are desiccated and shriveled to about half their normal size.

LENGTH: up to about 1.2 in.
HABITAT: gardens and moist forests.

Centipedes are predators, and they have venomous fangs that they use to subdue their prey. Our species are not dangerous to people, but small children should still avoid handling them. If you can get one to sit still for a moment, you'll see that each body segment carries one pair of legs, and the legs are set off to the sides. On a millipede, each segment bears two legs, set underneath.

CLOWN MILLIPEDE
Harpaphe haydeniana

The main similarity between a millipede and a centipede is that both their names end in "-ipede," a word root that refers to their feet. Millipedes are slow-moving animals that feed on plants or detritus. Big millipedes, at least in this part of the world, are bigger than big centipedes. The Clown Millipede is noteworthy because it produces cyanide as a defensive chemical. Some people call it the "almond-scented millipede," but the almond scent really comes from cyanide. The colors of this bug are warnings to would-be predators.

Millipedes have many more legs than a centipede—there are two pairs of legs per segment. With this many legs, they run the risk of getting in each other's way. So millipedes move their legs in slow, coordinated waves, starting at the back of the body and moving toward the head. Speaking of which, the antennae on a millipede's head give this creature a somewhat insect-like appearance from the neck forward, and, indeed, the science of animal classification places millipedes closer to insects than centipedes.

LENGTH: about 1.8 in.
HABITAT: forested areas with Douglas-fir.

For those who know that "millipede" means "1000 foot," while "centipede" means "100 foot," please note that millipedes always have fewer than 1000 feet, and centipedes can have as few as 30. A 100-footed centipede is actually an impossibility; they always have an odd number of leg pairs, giving either 49 × 2 = 98 or 51 × 2 = 102 legs in total.

141

SCORPION
Order Scorpionida

S corpions are tropical creatures, right? What then are they doing in the Pacific Northwest? Well, they do like warmth, so the only places you can find them here are in the drier, more desert-like parts of Washington and Oregon. The Mordant Scorpion (*Uroctonus mordax*) is our most common species. In Washington and Oregon there are perhaps as many as a half dozen species of scorpions. South of us, California has 40 species of scorpions, while to the north, Canada has only one.

Scorpions are unmistakable, with their pincer claws, eight walking legs and long abdomen with a sting at the end. Some scorpions from Arizona and nearby areas can be deadly venomous. The sting of our local species, however, is apparently not much worse than a hornet. Mind you, reports of the effect of our species' stings are few, and it's best not to take chances. Even if you spend time in their habitat, you will probably have trouble finding them. By day they stay under rocks. By night they hunt on the ground for other small bugs, and then you can find them with a flashlight. If you have a portable fluorescent camping light, try putting blacklight bulbs in it. Under the rays of ultraviolet light, scorpions glow with an eerie green color, making them much easier to spot.

LENGTH: usually about 1.4 in.
HABITAT: dry, open areas.

PSEUDOSCORPIONS
Order Pseudoscorpionida

The name "pseudoscorpion" means, literally, "false scorpion." However, it is unfair to characterize these amazing little creatures merely by comparison with their larger, more famous relatives. Pseudoscorpions look like real scorpions in miniature, except that they do not have a stinger. In fact, their abdomen is blunt, much like that of a spider. Some Pseudoscorpions have eyes, and some do not. Like scorpions, they capture their prey with pincers, and in some species the pincers themselves (the "pedipalps") have poison glands within them, to help subdue smaller bugs. Pseudoscorpions also produce silk from their jaws; they use the silk to form shelters in which they can pass the dangerous periods of overwintering and molting into a new skin. The male also spins a silk mat when he is courting, on which he places a packet of sperm. The female picks up the sperm and uses it to fertilize her eggs. Like many

LENGTH: usually less than 0.2 in.
HABITAT: dry, open areas, under bark and in houses.

arachnids, these mothers are good parents. Most types keep their young in a brood pouch, where the young are fed by a secretion from the mother's body. Because the mothers rear relatively few young (a big brood contains 30), they are able to devote considerable attention to their babies, unlike most bugs, which produce hundreds or thousands of babies and then leave them to fend for themselves.

Most of these arachnids live in leaf litter or decaying wood, but some ride around on the bodies of large long-horned beetles, eating pesky mites and thereby helping their gigantic hosts.

CAMEL SPIDER
Family Eremobatidae

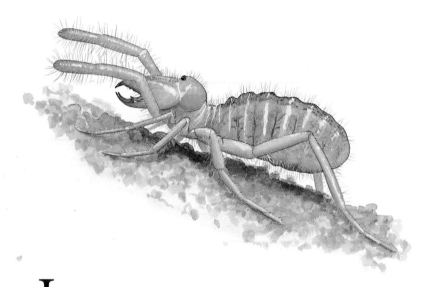

I t would be unfair to characterize these arachnids as psychopathic killers, but hey, that's what they look like to most people who have encountered one. These oddball critters have an eerie combination of spiderish legs, a thin-walled, bulbous abdomen, a bit of hairiness and a front end that is made up almost entirely of jaw-like pincers. These pincers are held in an up-and-down fashion, rather than side-to-side like most other bugs, and they make camel spiders look horrifically mammal-like when they chew. Their speckish eyes give no sense of intelligence whatsoever, and, indeed, camel spiders live mainly to kill other bugs.

LENGTH: about 0.9 in.
HABITAT: dry areas.

I suppose they also live to reproduce, and to their credit the mother camel spider guards her eggs for many weeks, and stays with the young until they complete their first molt. These spiders can be found in the same sorts of hot, dry habitats as scorpions. You will see these arachnids called "wind-scorpions," "solpugids," "camel spiders" and "sunspiders." I prefer "camel spider," the Arabian name, because we once had native camels in this part of the world, and these bugs watched the rise and fall of the North American camel, long before the arrival of civilization.

GARDEN HARVESTMAN
Order Opiliones

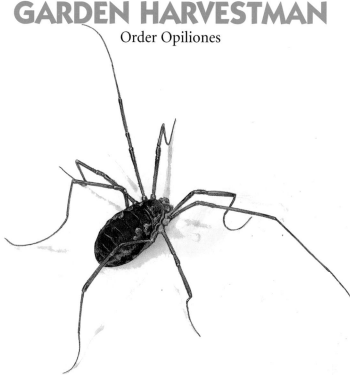

I used to call these creatures "daddy long-legs," and as a kid I thought they were spiders. I now try to use the more traditional name "Harvestman" to refer to them, because just about any long-legged bug gets called a daddy long-legs (crane flies especially). Harvestmen are not spiders. Spiders have two main body parts while harvestmen have no constriction

> **LENGTH:** about 0.2 in, without the legs.
> **HABITAT:** forests and gardens.

between the head and the abdomen. Harvestmen are also unable to produce silk. Their eyes are set in a little mound on the top of the body, and eight legs extend out from the sides.

These critters are predatory, although, as you might imagine, they are no match for anything but small prey. They will also scavenge on dead bugs or bits of decaying plants. Because they are such familiar garden bugs, various odd beliefs have developed about them. Some people believe that they are extremely venomous, even though it is tough to get them to bite. This belief is, as far as I can determine, complete baloney. Another weird idea says that if your cow goes missing, pull off a harvestman's leg and throw it on the ground, where it will point you in the right direction.

CAROLINA WOLF SPIDER

Lycosa carolinensis

W olf spiders are wandering hunters, and although they do not spin a web, they can still produce silk from the "spinneret" glands on their abdomen. Most of the time, you will see these spiders in grassy places, where they search for other bugs. They are easy to find day or night, and if you search for them with a head lamp (not a flashlight), you'll see their eyes gleaming in the grass, like little points of dew. The trick is to go out looking on a dry night when there is no dew to confuse you!

LENGTH: about 1 in.
HABITAT: drier areas with vegetation.

Wolf spiders have moderately good vision, and they can also see the patterns of polarized light in the sky, which helps them find their way around their grassy little worlds. Females are bigger than the males, and when they lay eggs, they wrap them in a silk bag. The bag is then attached to the spinnerets, and the female spider carries the eggs with her until they hatch—making her look like an even bigger spider with a blue abdomen, the blue part being, of course, the egg sac. When the young hatch, they cling to the body of the mother, holding onto special "handle" hairs on her back.

JOHNSON'S JUMPER
Phidippus johnsoni

E ven those with a deep-seated fear of spiders sometimes see a glimmer of cuteness in the members of the jumping spider family. Sure, they have eight legs and eight eyes, but they don't move in the same creepy way that other spiders do. Instead, they walk around in a more insect-

LENGTH: up to 0.4 in.
HABITAT: drier areas.

like fashion (if you know what I mean), and they also jump. When you look at one up close, most of the time it will turn and look back, with a pair of big bright eyes on the front of its head.

Jumping spiders have the best vision of any spider, and they can swivel their head around to examine whatever catches their interest. Add to these abilities the fact that some, like the Johnson's Jumper, have colorful bodies and iridescent fangs, and you have a spider with both a "face" and a personality. Many of the smaller male jumping spiders also do complicated little courtship dances, waving their fangs, their palps (the little leggish things in front of the fangs) and their front legs, like colored flags. If the female likes the dance, they will mate. These spiders are not aggressive, but the bite of the biggest ones (such as the Johnson's Jumper) can be painful and unsightly.

147

SIX-SPOTTED FISHING SPIDER

Dolomedes triton

I f you read a lot of nature books, you'll eventually see pictures of these spiders eating small fishes. Six-spotted Fishing Spiders live in ponds and can walk on the water like a water strider, although they let their heavy bellies lay on the surface because they can't quite support their weight on tiptoes. They can crawl around on underwater plants, breathing from air trapped in the tiny hairs that cover their body and legs. So it is quite natural that they would eat small fishes. However, I once worked in a lab where we studied these spiders, and none of the arachnologists I worked with ever saw one get a fish! The fishing spiders ate lots of water striders, damselflies and bugs that fell in the water but not one fish. Maybe these spiders catching fishes happens more often in other places, or maybe those photographs were posed.

LENGTH: females to 0.6 in; males to 0.4 in.
HABITAT: ponds.

Female fishing spiders are bigger than the males, and they often eat the males during or after courtship. Females who have already mated are less patient with suitors, so males sometimes follow immature females, waiting for them to reach adulthood. When the female lays her eggs, she carries them in a silk bag in her jaws, unlike wolf spiders (p.146), which carry them on their spinnerets.

GOLDENROD CRAB SPIDER

Misumena vatia

Here's the scenario: a big fat spider waits patiently in a fresh blossom. Sometimes the spider is yellow and sometimes it is white, and sometimes these colors blend in perfectly with the flowers, while other times they don't. An insect comes to the flower for a sip of nectar, and suddenly it becomes spider fodder.

My favorite story about this spider involved a butterfly, a western tailed blue. The blue was flitting about in the greenery, stopping from time to time to sun itself, when it spied another blue. It flapped over to investigate, but the second butterfly seemed completely uninterested. That's when I saw the female Goldenrod Crab Spider, tucked up between the purple flowers of the vetch they all were on. Before the first blue could comprehend the situation (if ever it could at all), the spider reached out, grabbed it and had two blues for lunch instead of one. Not only had the spider used the flower as an ambush, it had also used the first blue as a decoy!

LENGTH: females about 0.3 in; males about 0.1 in.
HABITAT: meadows and clearings.

Males of this species are smaller than the females and are darker in color. In a wild rose flower, they look almost exactly like the pollen-bearing stamens—the best buggy camouflage I know of in this part of the world.

BLACK WIDOW
Lactrodectus hesperus

Black Widows in the Pacific Northwest? Absolutely! However, they are much easier to find in drier areas and not really common in the places where most people live. The best way to see one is to walk around in mid-summer, and shine a flashlight down old mammal burrows. The Black Widow spins a disorganized web, and it is just about the easiest spider in the Pacific Northwest to identify: shiny black with a red hourglass on its tummy. The False Black Widows (*Steatoda* spp.) are more brownish and not as large.

LENGTH: females to 0.5 in; males to 0.2 in.
HABITAT: dry areas.

The venom of these beasts can indeed be deadly, but fortunately they are shy and docile most of the time. Females do eat the males quite often after mating, but this practice is actually fairly common among spiders, and it is not the macabre ritual that some people imagine. Apart from mammal burrows, old buildings and log piles, the best place to look for Black Widows is in the grocery store, because many of them come in along with fruits and vegetables. Sometimes they have red or orange markings on their backs, indicating they came from the southern states.

YELLOW GARDEN SPIDER

Argiope aurantia

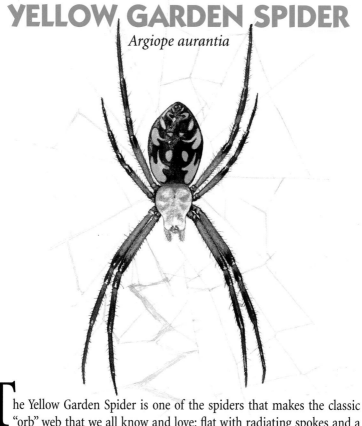

The Yellow Garden Spider is one of the spiders that makes the classic "orb" web that we all know and love: flat with radiating spokes and a spiral of silk connecting them together. If you have never watched a spider make a web, you really owe it to yourself to do so. If nothing else, it is fascinating to think of how wondrous it is that any animal could do something so complex based on nothing but pre-programmed instinct. As one of the few animals with almost no innate behavior patterns (except perhaps things like smiling or yawning), we really can't imagine what it is like.

LENGTH: up to 0.6 in.
HABITAT: gardens and shrubby places.

The spider spins a perfect web every time and knows exactly how to get around on it, holding the non-sticky threads while the prey get caught in the sticky ones.

Tossing small insects into an orb-weaver's web is standard practice for outdoor kids, and we've all seen the spider wrap up its prey in silk and then deliver the death-fanging that injects the poison. It is all the more exciting to watch when the spider is a great big Yellow Garden Spider.

LONG-BODIED CELLAR SPIDER

Pholcus phalangioides

T his bug is yet another one that commonly goes by the name "daddy long-legs," along with "harvestmen," "crane flies" and who knows what else. I much prefer the name "Long-bodied Cellar Spider." These weird spiders live in dark, musty places like the back corners of basements, attics and garages. They must be incredibly patient, waiting for some other bug to wander into such an unlikely place for a trap. The web of this species is roughly horizontal, but it is very messy and sometimes more three-dimensional than two-dimensional. Long-bodied Cellar Spiders are also found in Europe, where the cellar was invented, I suppose. They have been with us in North America for so long, no one knows for sure if they are native here or not. Perhaps they stowed away in dank corners of dark, musty ships.

LENGTH: about 0.3 in (body length), with legs up to 2 in.
HABITAT: dark, quiet places in buildings.

Of course, we don't see these spiders while they sit for weeks or months alone, waiting for a meal. We see them when we suddenly turn on the light and startle them. Then, the Long-bodied Cellar Spider does something really neat. It starts swinging around in its web like a crazed gymnast, whirring back and forth so fast on the elastic web strands that you can't possibly follow it with your eyes. I wonder if they practice that in the dark when no one is looking?

BOOKS FOR BUGSTERS

Unlike birds or mammals, there is no one book that covers the entire bug fauna of the Pacific Northwest or any other state, province or country, for that matter. You must be ready to face the fact that we have a great deal of knowledge about a few selected groups of bugs and almost no knowledge of all the others.

It is sad that almost all the references that follow are out of print or hard to get hold of. Let's hope that the work of detailing our arthropod fauna grows more and more vibrant in the new millennium, whether it is led by amateurs or professionals, or people like me, on the border between the two. Only then will up-to-date references become generally available.

The following books will take you a few steps further in your understanding of local bugs. I have avoided isolated papers in entomological journals, but if you are serious in your quest, these references will quickly lead you to them as well.

You might also try searching the worldwide web for information on specific sorts of bugs. As usual, some of it is well-researched and helpful, while most is not. Some groups, such as dragonflies, enjoy much better coverage on the web than others.

Books

Arnett, Ross H., Jr. 1985. *American Insects: A Handbook of the Insects of America North of Mexico*. Van Nostrand Reinhold Company, New York.

Bartlett Wright, Amy. 1993. *Peterson First Guide to Caterpillars of North America*. Houghton Mifflin Co., Boston and New York.

Chu, H.F., and Laurence K. Cutkomp. 1992. *How to Know the Immature Insects*. Pictured Key Nature Series. Wm. C. Brown Publishers, Dubuque, Iowa.

Dornfield, Ernest J. 1980. *The Butterflies of Oregon*. Timber Press. Forest Grove, Oregon.

Furniss, R.L., and V.M. Carolin. 1977. *Western Forest Insects*. U.S. Department of Agriculture, Forest Service. Miscellaneous Publications, No. 1339.

Gordon, Robert. 1985. *The Coccinellidae (Coleoptera) of North America North of Mexico. Journal of the New York Entomological Society*, Volume 93, No. 1.

Hatch, Melvin H. 1953–71. *The Beetles of the Pacific Northwest. Parts I–V.* University of Washington Press, Seattle.

Holland, W.J. 1968. *The Moth Book.* Dover Publications Inc., New York.

Jaques, H.E. 1951. *How to Know the Beetles.* Wm. C. Brown Publishers, Dubuque, Iowa.

Kaston, B.J. 1978. *How to Know the Spiders.* Pictured Key Nature Series. Wm. C. Brown Publishers, Dubuque, Iowa.

Opler, Paul A., and Amy Bartlett Wright. 1999. *A Field Guide to Western Butterflies.* Peterson Field Guide Series. Houghton Mifflin Co., New York.

Otte, Daniel. 1981. *North American Grasshoppers.* Volume 1. Harvard University Press.

———. 1984. *North American Grasshoppers.* Volume 2. Harvard University Press.

Paulson, Dennis. 1999. *Dragonflies of Washington.* Seattle Audubon Society, Seattle.

Pyle, Robert Michael. 1974. *Watching Washington Butterflies.* Seattle Audubon Society, Seattle.

———. 1981. *The Audubon Society Field Guide to North American Butterflies.* Alfred A. Knopf, New York.

———. 1992. *Handbook for Butterfly Watchers.* Houghton Mifflin Co., Boston and New York.

Shaw, John. 1987. *John Shaw's Closeups in Nature: The Photographer's Guide to Techniques in the Field.* AMPHOTO, New York.

Usinger, Robert L., ed. 1956. *Aquatic Insects of California, with Keys to the North American Genera and Californian Species.* University of California Press, Berkeley and Los Angeles.

Westfall, Minter J., Jr., and Michael L. May. 1996. *Damselflies of North America.* Scientific Publishers, Gainesville, Florida.

White, Richard E. 1983. *A Field Guide to the Beetles of North America.* Peterson Field Guide Series. Houghton Mifflin Co., New York.

Other Information

The following is the contact information for various societies that can help you further your interest in bugs and enhance your enjoyment of the subject. Some organizations are local, and some are worldwide, but all have publications and meetings:

American Arachnological Society: c/o Norman I. Platnick, Membership Secretary. Department of Entomology, American Museum of Natural History, Central Park West at 79th Street, New York, New York, 10024.

Coleopterists' Society: contact the society's treasurer, currently Terry Seeno, CDFA-PPD, 3294 Meadowview Road, Sacramento, California, 95832-1448. e-mail: <tseeno@ns.net>.

Dragonfly Society of the Americas: c/o T. Donnelly, 2091 Partridge Lane, Binghamton, New York, 13903. website: <http://www.afn.org/~iori/dsaintro.html>.

Lepidopterists' Society: c/o Los Angeles County Museum, 900 Exposition Boulevard, Los Angeles, California, 90007-4057. website: <http://www.furman.edu/~snyder/snyder/lep/>.

North American Butterfly Association: 4 Delaware Road, Morristown, New Jersey, 07960. website: <http://www.naba.org>.

Oregon Entomological Society: c/o Oregon State University, Department of Entomology, Cordley Hall #2046, Corvalis, Oregon, 97331-2907.

Washington State Entomological Society: Department of Entomology, Washington State University, Pullman, Washington, 99164-6382.

Young Entomologists' Society: 1915 Peggy Place, Lansing, Michigan, 48910-2553. website: <http://insects.ummz.lsa.umich.edu/yes/yes.html>. e-mail: <YESbugs@aol.com>.

And finally, for entomological supplies and/or books, contact

Bio Quip Inc.: 17803 LaSalle Avenue, Gardena, California, 90248-3602. phone: (310) 324 0620, fax (310) 324 7931. e-mail: <bioquip @aol.com>.

INDEX

Page numbers in **boldface** type refer to the primary, illustrated accounts.

ABOUT THE AUTHOR

Since the age of five, John Acorn has been hopelessly fascinated by insects—a benign affliction that eventually led to a Master's degree in Entomology from the University of Alberta. His thesis work focused on tiger beetles, which are still among his favorite insects. Today, he works as an award-winning freelance writer, speaker and broadcaster, and he is best known as "Acorn, The Nature Nut," host of an international television series. John spends most of his spare time being exactly what you might expect—a bugster. He is also the author of Lone Pine's *Birds of the Pacific Northwest Coast*.

ABOUT THE ILLUSTRATOR

Ian Sheldon has been captivated by bugs since the age of three. Born in Edmonton, Ian later lived in South Africa, England and Singapore. Exposure to nature from so many different places enhanced his desire to study bugs and other creatures further, and he earned an award from the Zoological Society of London and a degree from Cambridge University. He has also completed a Master's degree in Ecotourism Development, which involved research in Thailand. Ian is an accomplished artist represented by galleries internationally, and he is both a writer and illustrator of many other nature guides, including Lone Pine's *Seashore of Northern and Central California*, *Animal Tracks of Washington and Oregon* and *Animal Tracks of Northern California*.